How to
with
VAT
Third edition

How to live with VAT

Third edition

An easy-to-follow guide, including tax saving hints for small and medium-size businesses

John Brooks BA (Hons.)
and
Andrew Copp LL B (Hons.)

McGRAW-HILL BOOK COMPANY

London · New York · St Louis · San Francisco · Auckland · Bogotá
Guatemala · Hamburg · Lisbon · Madrid · Mexico · Montreal
New Delhi · Panama · Paris · San Juan · São Paulo · Singapore
Sydney · Tokyo · Toronto

Published by
McGRAW-HILL Book Company (UK) Limited
MAIDENHEAD · BERKSHIRE · ENGLAND

British Library Cataloguing in Publication Data
Brooks, John
 How to live with VAT: an easy-to-follow guide, including tax saving hints for small and medium-size businesses. – 3rd ed
 1 Great Britain. Value-added tax
 I. Title II. Copp, Andrew
 336.2'714'0941

 ISBN 0–07–707307–X

Copyright © 1989 McGraw-Hill Book Company (UK) Limited. All rights reserved. No part of this publication may be reproduced, stored in a retrieval system, or transmitted, in any form or by any means, electronic, mechanical, photocopying, recording, or otherwise, without the prior permission of McGraw-Hill Book Company (UK) Limited.

1234 B&S 8909

Typeset by Computape (Pickering) Ltd, North Yorkshire
Printed and bound in Great Britain by Billing & Sons Ltd, Worcester

To our families

Contents

	Preface	ix
	Acknowledgements	x
1	What is VAT and how does it work?	1
2	Who must register for VAT?	7
3	When liability arises	17
4	How the amount of VAT is calculated	29
5	Issuing invoices	34
6	When is VAT due?	37
7	When the debtor does not pay	39
8	Exporting goods and services	41
9	Special schemes for retailers	45
10	Second-hand goods	65
11	Claiming back VAT	71
12	VAT and the importer	78
13	The partly exempt business	82
14	Records and accounts	86
15	Completing returns	90
16	Your legal rights and obligations	95
17	Using the Tribunal	109
18	Goodbye to all VAT	119
	Index	127

Preface

How to live with VAT was conceived at a time when there were very few books published about VAT. Throughout the seventies and into the eighties the 'little blue books' and leaflets published by Customs and Excise were the only survival guides business people had to rely on. These became the VAT bibles. Unfortunately they suffer from the drawbacks of most scriptures in that the language they are written in is sometimes difficult to follow and their viewpoint is somewhat one sided. More recently several worthy technical books on VAT have appeared on the market but these are aimed more at the tax specialist and practitioner than the business community.

How to live with VAT fills a much needed gap. It is written with busy business people in mind and explains the VAT system in an easy to understand way, avoiding technicalities as much as possible. Starting with an introduction to VAT language and the bureaucracy of VAT it sets out, chapter by chapter, the problems likely to be faced by a small to medium sized business from the first requirements to register for VAT, through to what to do on giving up or selling a business. The book has been completely revised to incorporate the most important recent changes in VAT brought in by the 1989 Finance Act.

Acknowledgements

The authors would like to thank Stephen Copp, LL B, Barrister-at-Law for his valuable contribution in writing the section on abuse of powers.

CHAPTER ONE

What is VAT and how does it work?

Value Added Tax (VAT) is a tax added to the value of goods and services that are supplied by persons (including partnerships and limited companies) carrying on a business and who are required to be registered for VAT. Not every person who supplies goods and services has to be registered. Some will have to because of the size of their turnover. Sometimes it is beneficial to register voluntarily. Only supplies made in the course of a business give rise to a VAT liability and only when the supply is made in the United Kingdom. The law governing VAT lays down rules for determining where a supply of goods and services takes place. For VAT purposes, the United Kingdom includes the area of sea within the twelve-mile limit around the coast.

Not all transactions are made in the course of a business. Such transactions are not supplies for VAT purposes and do not give rise to any VAT liability. For example, employees are not themselves carrying on a business, so wages are not subject to VAT.

All goods and services (supplies) are at present either:

a Liable to VAT at 15%; or
b Liable to VAT at a zero rate; or
c Exempt from VAT

b and **c** at first seem the same (no VAT) but there are important differences. Although both zero rated and exempt supplies carry no VAT charge there is a legal difference between the two categories. Zero rated supplies are included in turnover for VAT registration purposes, whereas exempt supplies are not. Furthermore if you only make exempt supplies you will not be able to reclaim VAT charged to you when you purchase goods and services for your business purposes.

If you are registered, you must comply with the law on VAT. You will have to send in VAT returns (usually 4 times a year) and forward any VAT you owe. Failure to obtain mandatory registration can have serious results.

On your VAT returns you must declare all the VAT due on the supplies you have made (output tax). Against this you can offset the VAT on the purchases you have made for your business (input tax). You pay the balance due to Customs and Excise when you send in your VAT return, or claim it back if your input tax exceeds your output tax.

Periodically you will be visited by Customs and Excise officials who will inspect your books and records.

Isle of Man

The Isle of Man has a common VAT system with the United Kingdom and the two countries are effectively the same territory for VAT purposes. The rules described in this book are equally applicable in the Isle of Man. Although Manx VAT is administered separately, if a business is registered for VAT in the Isle of Man it is not required to register for VAT in the United Kingdom and vice versa. If a business is established in both countries Customs and Excise in the United Kingdom will determine in which country it is to be registered.

Administration of VAT

The Civil Service department responsible for collecting and administering VAT is HM Customs and Excise. It has a special section for VAT with many local offices and a controlling computer centre at Southend-on-Sea, called the VAT Central Unit (VCU). Local offices deal with routine queries, and it is officers from these who will visit you from time to time to inspect your accounts and records. The local offices usually deal with the initial stages in collecting unpaid tax.

The VCU will issue the VAT returns and process them when you send them back. It receives payments and issues repayments.

However, we cannot rigidly define the duties of the local offices and VCU, and there is much inter-action and liaison between them.

It might help you to follow the system better if we use a few diagrams. To know and understand what and who you are dealing with often helps remove initial worries.

VAT from top to bottom

Your local VAT office will be listed with its address in the telephone directory under 'Customs and Excise'.

Control districts

These are units of officers who cover a certain geographical area for the purpose of inspecting businesses' accounts and records.

Enforcement

This section deals with the initial stages of collecting overdue tax, e.g. by written request, and also by visiting businesses with bailiffs to remove goods to the value of unpaid VAT.

Local Investigation Branch

These branches deal with cases of a more serious nature, e.g. fraud.

VAT language—what it all means

Some of the more important expressions used for VAT are explained below.

EC

The European Community includes the territories of Belgium, Denmark, France, West Germany, Greece, Ireland, Italy, Luxemburg, The Netherlands, Portugal, Spain and the United Kingdom.

Diagram 1

COMMISSIONERS OF CUSTOMS AND EXCISE

| Central Investigation Branch | V.C.U.  | Solicitors office (For all legal matters, e.g. liquidations; prosecutions) |

Local Offices—L.V.O.'s (Local VAT Offices)

Sub Offices—V.S.O.'s (VAT Sub Offices mainly rural and very small)

Diagram 2

THE LOCAL VAT OFFICE

ENQUIRIES SECTION

| REGISTRATION SECTION | DEREGISTRATION SECTION |

| 1 | 2 | 3 | 4 | 5 |

CONTROL DISTRICTS

ENFORCEMENT AND PROSECUTION SECTION

LOCAL INVESTIGATION BRANCH

Diagram 3

Who does what in the VAT Office

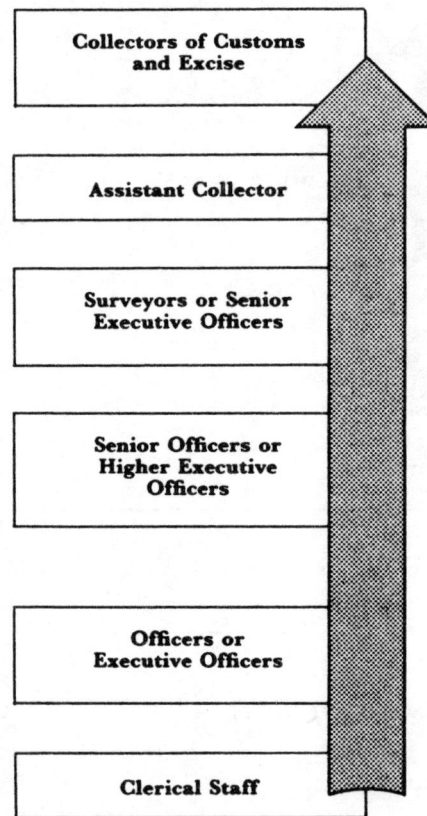

Collectors and their deputies control collection of VAT and other Customs and Excise duties in the area.

The assistant collector is in control of the local VAT office.

One of these is usually in charge of a control district, perhaps the enforcement section or the enquiries section.

There are usually two or more officers for each control district in charge of visiting officers. They also deal with more difficult cases. Two officers are usually found in the enforcement section.

These officers often visit traders to inspect accounts and collect unpaid tax. One or two are usually in the general enquiries section. Five or more could be found in a control district or enforcement section.

Exempt; exemptions
Certain types of goods and services are exempt from VAT. They are relieved from VAT when supplied but the supplier is not able to reclaim VAT on his costs. Exempt goods and services are listed in the VAT Act 1983, Schedule 6. A person who makes taxable and exempt supplies is termed partly exempt and is able to recover only a part of his input tax.

Inputs and input tax
Your purchases and other incoming supplies which you incur for business purposes are called inputs. The VAT on them is input tax.

(i) Deductible input tax
   This is input tax which is reclaimable as a business expense.

(ii) Non-deductible input tax
This is input tax which is not reclaimable.

Liability
This is the term used to describe whether or not a transaction is subject to VAT.

Outputs and output tax
The sales and supplies you make are called outputs. The VAT on them is the output tax.

Outside the scope
Activities which do not involve making supplies in the course of business (i.e. are neither taxable nor exempt) are often referred to as being outside the scope of VAT. Outside the scope income includes donations received by charities, rates levied by local authorities, certain statutory charges such as DoT tests, and amounts received as damages or compensation for losses incurred or receipt of sums claimed against insurance. VAT is not payable on such sums. Subscriptions to political, religious, philanthropic, philosophical and patriotic organizations are also outside the scope of VAT.

Retail schemes
The name given to the different schemes that VAT registered retailers must use to calculate output tax due on retail sales.

Reverse charge
Businesses have to account for VAT (output tax) on payments for certain kinds of services received from overseas suppliers. This VAT is often referred to as the reverse charge. Its intention is to ensure that businesses do not gain a tax advantage by using overseas suppliers instead of suppliers based in the United Kingdom.

Self supply
The concept of self supply is peculiar to VAT. It is intended to ensure that persons in business who are not entitled to recover input tax do not obtain a tax advantage by producing goods and services in-house. The person producing the goods or services is treated as if he had supplied them to himself and so has to account for the tax on the self supply on his VAT returns. Self supply rules apply to stationery produced by exempt or partly exempt persons, motor cars and motor car conversions, and buildings used other than for the purpose of making taxable supplies.

Standard rate
All goods and services supplied in the United Kingdom in the course of as business are liable to the standard rate of VAT unless exempt or zero rated. The standard rate of VAT has been 15% since 18 June 1979.

Supply
This is the term used to describe the sale or other provision of goods and services made in the course of running a business.

Tax point
The term used to state the time when a supply takes place for VAT purposes.

Taxable person

A person who makes or intends to make taxable supplies and who is either registered for VAT, or required to be registered for VAT because his taxable turnover exceeds the VAT registration limits. A person includes a legal person, partnership or a members' association carrying on a business.

Taxable supply

A term used to describe the supply of goods and services which are not exempt from VAT.

Turnover

The total value of the supplies you make in any given period. The total value of your taxable supplies is often referred to as taxable turnover.

Zero rate

Another form of relief from VAT for business supplies. Unlike exempt supplies, zero rated supplies give the supplier the right to reclaim input tax on his costs and expenses. Exports of goods from the United Kingdom are zero rated, and goods and services listed in the VAT Act 1983, Schedule 5.

CHAPTER TWO

Who must register for VAT?

Firstly, it must be stressed that it is not the *business* that is registered, but the *person* carrying on that business. A person will include a sole proprietor, the partners of a partnership or a limited company. Clubs, charities, and other unincorporated institutions, will usually have to nominate a responsible officer to take on the duties of VAT registration and subsequent administration. All business activities of the person count in deciding whether or not he should be registered. Therefore if an individual carries on two separate businesses, the results of both must be merged to establish liability for registration. It may be possible to subdivide a business into separate business activities run by different legal persons, in order to keep the turnover of each or one of the activities below the limits for VAT registration. In doing so you must be able to show that the separate activities are in fact owned by different persons, and are in fact run independently of each other, eg separate records, financial accounts, and bank accounts should be kept. You should also be able to show that supplies between the two businesses are actually recorded. For example where a farm is registered for VAT in the name of a husband, or both husband or wife as a partnership, it may be possible for the wife to run an independent bed and breakfast business in the farmhouse and avoid VAT registration, as long as the above points are borne in mind.

However, Customs and Excise now have the power to direct persons party to such business splitting arrangements to unified registration in circumstances where the business splitting scheme has been adopted for the purpose of avoiding VAT.

They may exercise this power where it is reasonable to assume that the business activities should be regarded as part and parcel of a single business unit. This power has been given to prevent artificial arrangements merely designed to avoid paying VAT where the arrangements have no basis in ordinary business considerations.

An appeal against such a direction may be made to a VAT Tribunal (see Chapter 17).

Registration can be divided into two categories:
a Compulsory registration.
b Voluntary registration.

Compulsory registration

You are already trading and not registered
If you come under this heading you must consider whether you are obliged to register by law. You must consider two possibilities:
a Are there grounds to believe your taxable turnover will exceed £23,600 in the

coming year? If so, registration will take effect from the commencement of the year.

b You must look to your past taxable turnover.

From 15 March 1989 the taxable turnover limit for compulsory registration is £23,600 per annum or £8,000 per calendar quarter.

There are rules to decide whether you must be registered on the basis of past turnover. If in a quarter ending on 31 March, 30 June, 30 September, or 31 December your taxable turnover exceeds £8,000, you should 'notify' the local VAT office within 30 days of the end of the quarter. However, this does not necessarily mean that you have to register. You may avoid registration if you can satisfy the VAT office that the turnover will not exceed £23,600 for the whole year. This is often the case with seasonal trades, or where there is a one-off large contract with no reason to expect a repetition. Before 15 March 1989 the annual turnover limit was £22,100. Before 16 March 1988 the turnover limit was £21,300. Before 20 March 1985 tests for registration were different and turnover limits lower. Details are available from your local VAT office.

On application to the VAT office you will receive a registration form (VAT 1). A copy of form VAT 1 is reproduced overleaf. This is relatively straightforward to complete. You will be registered with effect from the end of the month following the quarter in which your turnover exceeds £8,000, or earlier by agreement with the VAT office. So, it is important that you keep a careful watch on your quarterly turnover and register promptly if necessary, otherwise you may be liable for VAT on your sales, when you have not charged it to your customers. If you do find yourself in this position you may request the VAT from your customers (although of course they are not obliged to pay) by issuing another invoice for the VAT at 15%. This should be no difficult task if the customer is VAT registered and able to claim back the 15% he is charged as a deductible business expense. If the tax cannot be recovered in this way then tax due on the sales where VAT should have been charged is calculated inclusively, i.e. the charges you have made to your customer are deemed to equal the VAT exclusive value of your goods and services plus the VAT itself. The VAT is found by multiplying the charge to the customer by the VAT fraction i.e.

$$\frac{15}{100+15} = \frac{3}{23}$$

For example if the charge made to a customer was £460 with no addition for VAT, and tax is at the rate of 15%, the output tax becomes

$$\frac{3}{23} \times £460 = £60$$

Thus £60 represents 15% of the tax exclusive price, namely £400.

In addition should you fail to register at the appropriate time, Customs and Excise can impose heavy penalties on you for the failure, up to 30% of any tax due up to the time they are notified (see Chapter 16).

You are not yet trading and not VAT registered

Here you cannot look to your turnover to consider whether or not you should be registered by applying the tests outlined above.

You will be immediately registered and given a VAT number if there are reasonable grounds to believe that your turnover will exceed the VAT registration limit in the forthcoming year. This will depend on surrounding evidence, e.g. perhaps the previous owner was registered because his turnover exceeded the limit.

VAT must be charged by you as soon as you *should* be registered. However, if you have not received your VAT number from the VAT Office you cannot show VAT separately on invoices you issue, as a VAT invoice must record your VAT number. So, if you have to issue invoices including VAT but cannot show it separately you should keep a log of such invoices showing the VAT you have charged. This will be accountable as output tax

Also, if customers are themselves registered for VAT they will want a correct VAT invoice when you receive your VAT registration number, in order that they may reclaim the VAT which they have paid to you. This makes for extra work and it is therefore advisable to act promptly in completing registration forms.

Voluntary registration

This arises where you cannot be compelled to register for VAT by law, as your turnover is under the VAT registration limits, but you may want to register voluntarily because it is in your own interests to do so. Examples of such instances are:

i If you will be in a repayment situation, i.e. your sales are mainly zero rated, but many of your business expenses are liable to VAT, e.g. farming and fishing.
ii Where customers are VAT registered and may be reluctant to deal with suppliers who are not.

Since a change in the law from 28 July 1988, voluntary registration is a right open to traders. Before this it was at the discretion of Customs and Excise.

Other registration issues

Registration before trading commences

This may be effected as long as you *intend* to trade. You must be able to satisfy Customs and Excise as to this intention by drawing on any surrounding evidence, e.g. contracts you have concluded or are negotiating or proof of expenses incurred towards setting up the business.

This sort of registration gives the benefit of repayment of VAT every month or quarter before the obligation to register for VAT arises.

Purchases made before date of registration

You may reclaim VAT on goods purchased before the date of registration provided that they are still used in the business at the time of registration.

Regarding services, you may only claim VAT on services received up to six months previous to registration, provided the services were not work carried out on goods disposed of prior to registering for VAT.

The VAT is reclaimed on the first VAT return. You must keep invoices to support your claim, and record details of purchases and disposals.

If you form a limited company, VAT incurred prior to incorporation may be reclaimed, subject to the above rules, if the purchases were made for the business by a person, who after incorporation, becomes a director, employee or person in a similar capacity and providing the person is reimbursed for his expense by the company.

Exemption from registration if turnover is all or mostly at the zero rate

If all or most of your supplies are zero rated and you only incur small amounts of VAT on your purchases, then Customs and Excise may exempt you from registration,

VALUE ADDED TAX — Application for Registration

HM Customs and Excise

For official use

- Date of receipt
- Local office code and registration number
- Name
- Trade name
- Taxable turnover
- EDR
- Rept. | Vol | Oversize name address | Computer user | Group Div. | Intg. | Overseas
- Bn

You should open up this form and read the notes before you answer these questions. Please write clearly in ink.

Applicant and business

1. Full name: ANDREW NEILL OTHER

2. Trading name: SOMETHING DIFFERENT

3. Address: 11 HIGH STREET, ANYTOWN, BLANKSHIRE

Phone no.: 012 - 76543

Postcode: BL1 99XX

4. Status of business

- Limited company ☐ — Company incorporation certificate no. _____ and date __/__/19__
- Sole proprietor ✓
- Partnership ☐
- Other-specify _____

5. Business activity: BOOK PUBLISHER

Trade classification: 4 8 9 1

6. Computer user: ✓

Repayments of VAT

7. ✓ Bank sorting code and account no.: 33 99 66 — 00 19 91 11

National Girobank account no.: _____

VAT 1

please continue overleaf ⟶

Compulsory registrations

8 Date of first taxable supply — day `1` month `11` year `1989`

Value of taxable supplies in the 12 months from that date. £ **500,000**

9 Date from which you have to be registered — day `1` month `11` year `1989`

10 Exemption from compulsory registration ☐

expected value of zero-rated supplies in the next 12 months £ _____

Other types of registration

11 Taxable supplies below registration limits ☐

value of taxable supplies in the last 12 months £ _____

12 No taxable supplies made yet ☐

(a) expected annual value of taxable supplies £ _____

(b) expected date of first taxable supply — day ___ month ___ year `19`

Business changes and transfers

13 Business transferred as a going concern ✓

(a) date of transfer or change of legal status — day `1` month `11` year `1989`

(b) name of previous owner — **SMART MOVE LTD**

(c) previous VAT registration number (if known) — `1 2 3 4 5 6 7 8 9`

14 Transfer of VAT registration number ☐

Related businesses

15 Other VAT registrations — Yes ☐ No ☐

Declaration — You must complete this declaration.

16 I **ANDREW NEILL OTHER**
(Full name in BLOCK LETTERS)
declare that all the entered details and information in any accompanying documents are correct and complete.

Signature *A N Other*   Date `1 October 1989`

Proprietor ✓   Partner ☐   Director ☐   Company Secretary ☐   Authorised Official ☐   Trustee ☐

For official use

Registration	Obligatory	Exemption	Voluntary	Intending	Transfer of Regn. no.
Approved — Initial/Date					
Refused — Initial/Date					
Form Issued — Initial/Date	VAT 9/ Other	VAT 8	VAT 7	Letter	Approval Letter

VAT 1 F3733(APRIL 1988)

11

Monitoring turnover for VAT registration purposes

Example 1 Growing trading pattern
Starting business 1 January 1989, from scratch, not knowing what turnover is likely to be:

Month	Turnover Monthly (£)	Quarterly (£)	Accumulating total (£)	What to do
January February March	2,000 2,000 2,500	6,500	6,500	No need to register yet. Quarterly turnover less than £8,000.
April May June	2,000 2,250 2,750	7,000	13,500	No need to register yet. But look at next quarter's turnover carefully. Quarterly turnover is approaching £8,000.
July August September	2,500 2,500 2,750	7,750	21,250	Quarterly turnover still is not more than £8,000 but if trading pattern continues then turnover for next twelve months will exceed £23,600. If you have grounds for believing this then you must inform the VAT Office before 30 October. The business will be registered as from 31 October.

Note: Before 15 March 1989 the quarterly limit was £7,500 and the annual limit was £22,100.

Example 2 Seasonal trading pattern

Month	Turnover (£) Month	Turnover (£) Quarterly	Accumulating total	What to do
January February March	Closed Closed Closed	Nil	Nil	No need to register.
April May June	1,000 2,000 3,000	6,000	6,000	No need to register yet. Quarterly turnover below £8,000.
July August September	4,000 4,000 3,000	11,000	17,000	Inform VAT Office that this quarter's turnover exceeds £8,000, but that the annual figure is likely to be below £23,600 because of seasonal nature of trade.
October November December	2,000 Closed Closed	2,000	19,000	No need to register. Annual turnover below £23,600.

13

if you so wish. The reasons are self-evident; the Customs and Excise save on both repayment and the internal administration costs. From the business proprietor's point of view this could mean a saving in time and the cost of keeping records for little gain.

However, VAT registration forms must still be completed as this exemption is at the discretion of the Customs and Excise.

Residence and registration

If you are not a resident of the UK you may be confronted with special rules that determine whether or not you have to register for VAT. Liability to register largely depends on where the supply is made. This is because supplies of goods and services in the UK are subject to VAT law. In general a supply of goods takes place in the country where the goods are when the contract to sell and supply is made. However a supply of services takes place in the country where the supplier belongs, eg where there exists a business establishment closely connected with the supply, such as an office or works.

If you are not resident or do not have a presence in the UK and you are making supplies here, for example sales of goods from your own stocks held in the UK, someone in the UK must be responsible for your VAT registration. This may be an agent acting on your behalf. Customs and Excise no longer insist on an agent being given power of attorney before he can take responsibility for an overseas person's VAT registration.

Group registration of limited companies

A group of companies may be registered under one collective registration if it can be shown they are under the control of one company or person or two or more people acting in partnership together. To be included in a VAT group a company must be resident in the United Kingdom. The VAT registration may cover the entire group of companies or it may be confined to only a few of the group members. The main effect of group registration is to exclude transactions between members from VAT liability. This may make savings on administrative time, and expense and improve cashflow. The group is treated as a single person and one member is responsible for the VAT administration.

Careful planning is necessary to determine which companies to include in the group and which companies to exclude from it. It may be desirable to exclude companies from the group which make high exempt outputs to non-group members. To include such a company in the group could make the entire group partly exempt, which would affect the amount of input tax the entire group could claim (see Chapter 13).

However, it may be beneficial to include in the group a company which makes high exempt outputs to other group members. As inter-group transactions are ignored for VAT purposes, the input tax of the exempt company may be recovered by the group where it would not if the exempt company were registered on its own account.

Refusals to grant an application to join a VAT group

Customs and Excise may refuse an application by a company to form or join a VAT group with another if it appears necessary for the protection of the revenue. The phrase 'for the protection of the revenue' does not appear to have been defined in law so we cannot be certain whether it applies only to schemes which set out to defraud the revenue or whether it includes using the provision as a legitimate device to minimize a tax liability. The power to refuse a VAT group application on these grounds has been little used by Customs and Excise but they have made it clear that they will be applying their powers more widely in the future. It remains to be seen just how widely this power will be applied, and whether the courts have a different view on the extent of its application. A refusal by Customs to include a company in a VAT group can be appealed against. Customs and Excise do not have any power to refuse an application by a company to leave a VAT group.

Divisional registration for limited companies and other corporate bodies
A company which has a substructure consisting of divisions may apply for separate registration, for each division, although the company remains responsible for the VAT affairs of all the divisions. Divisional registration means each division has to be registered, irrespective of its turnover. Each division must be self-accounting, although transactions between divisions do not require the issue of VAT invoices.

Divisional registration will not be allowed if the company is partly exempt (see Chapter 13).

Registration of persons not making taxable supplies in the United Kingdom
Certain classes of persons can register for VAT even though they may not make taxable supplies in the course of a business in the UK. In order to register for VAT the person must show that:
1 he either has a business establishment or is resident in the United Kingdom;
2 he does not make (or intend to make) taxable supplies in the UK;
3 he makes supplies outside the UK which would be taxable had they been made in the UK, or supplies goods in a bonded warehouse.

This provision enables individuals and companies on certain classes of business overseas or in a bonded warehouse to register for VAT and claim back input tax on their expenses. It takes the place of a previous more limited provision which allowed persons carrying on a business overseas to register for VAT. The provision was effective from 15 May 1987.

DIY builders scheme
If you are planning to build your own house, then you will want to take advantage of the DIY builders scheme. This entitles you to reclaim VAT on the materials you buy for constructing a house.

To qualify, you need not perform any of the manual tasks—you may employ skilled labour. As long as you are in charge of the building site and purchasing of materials you qualify as a builder.

The house or other dwelling you are building need not be for your own occupation—it may be intended for a relative or a friend—but it must not be built for business purposes, i.e. with the intention of selling it. It must be a dwelling and not any kind of business or industrial building (for which VAT registration may be necessary). The dwelling must be a completely new construction and not the result of converting an existing building from another use.

VAT may be reclaimed on all materials used for construction and standard fixtures and fittings, e.g. bathroom and kitchen fittings, built-in kitchen furniture and central hearing systems.

VAT may not be reclaimed on non-standard fittings, e.g., built-in-fridges, built-in washing machines and built-in cookers.

You will not be able to reclaim VAT on professional fees, i.e. architects', surveyors' and solicitors' fees, but the services of anyone engaged in the building, including bricklayers, carpenters, plumbers, electricians, etc., should be free of VAT.

You cannot reclaim VAT on the hire of equipment needed to construct your house.

But if the hire includes the services of an operator then the whole charge should be VAT free.

To make a claim you must obtain the special declaration forms from your local VAT office. Ask for VAT invoices from all your suppliers and keep them safe. They must be submitted with the claim. You must make a claim within three months of the completion of the dwelling. If Customs and Excise refuse a claim, in whole or in part, they must state why and you do have the right of appeal if you are dissatisfied with the answer.

If you are involved with a mutual housing association, ie a group of people who form an association to construct houses to sell to members, the association should be registered for VAT as a business in the normal way. You should register the association for VAT before the construction of houses begins. The normal VAT rules and regulations will apply to the association as they do to any ordinary business.

Self-help groups

A similar scheme to the DIY builders scheme exists for self-help groups, i.e. a group of individuals who set about building something of use to the community at large—e.g. a church hall, day centre. The rules as to what can and cannot be reclaimed are similar to the DIY builders scheme except self-help groups can claim back input tax on services supplied to them. A self-help group should apply for VAT registration before starting work, rather than make a claim in the DIY builders' way.

CHAPTER THREE

When liability arises

Liability to VAT
The law requires that all supplies of goods and services made by a registered person will be liable to VAT at the standard rate (currently 15%) unless some specific relief applies. In other words there is nothing to say that a particular item is liable to VAT at 15%, only that some goods and services are not.

Those goods and services that are not liable to VAT at the standard rate are listed under two schedules of the VAT Act 1983. One schedule lists supplies which are zero rated and the other deals with supplies which are exempt.

An item that is zero rated is supplied without any VAT charge but is otherwise treated as a supply liable to VAT. In other words, someone who makes only zero rated supplies can register for VAT and recover input tax incurred on business expenditure.

An item that is exempt from VAT is supplied without any VAT charge and does not count for VAT purposes. In other words, someone who makes *ONLY* exempt supplies cannot register for VAT, nor can that person obtain relief for input tax incurred on business expenses.

In the event of a second positive rate being introduced, a similar schedule will be enacted to include all supplies covered by the new rate. This happened when the higher rate schedule (now repealed) was brought in, during 1976.

These schedules are written by legal draughtsmen and are often vaguely worded. In their official booklets Customs and Excise reprint the schedules with explanatory notes; but their desire for caution sometimes leaves the businessman's question, on which he may have to make a decision, unanswered. It is little wonder, therefore, that the interpretation and application of these laws create unnecessary problems for businesses.

As a general rule, wholesalers and retailers are fairly safe when it comes to applying the standard rate or zero rate of VAT. They can charge out VAT on goods at the same rate charged by the manufacturer or distributor, in the reasonably certain knowledge that the latter will have sorted out any VAT liability problems with the Customs and Excise.

If you are in doubt about what rate of VAT to charge on a particular supply, contact your local VAT Office by telephone or letter. If the answer given does not seem to be an obvious one, write to them outlining the problem and request a written ruling. This is most important as written rulings are undeniable should problems occur at a later date.

Remember also that the Customs and Excise are not the final arbiters in these matters. If you are not satisfied with a decision they give you concerning the liability of supplies you make, you can appeal to a VAT Tribunal. You may be able to get advice on this from your solicitor or accountant. Local practices of the larger accountancy firms are able to refer problems to a VAT specialist working in larger city offices. You will have to pay more for the specialist's time, however, than your local accountant's. Beyond this, appeals lie to the High Court, and VAT cases are heard by

the Court of Appeal and the House of Lords. How far you are prepared to take the matter depends on:
a   how important the decision is in affecting your business;
b   your financial resources;
c   the leave of the Courts.

1988 and 1992
On 21 June 1988 the European Court of Justice delivered a judgment which served as a reminder that VAT is not simply a national tax but is collected as part of the United Kingdom's obligations as a member of the European Community (EC). As a result of that judgment the Government has introduced some major changes to the VAT liability of certain supplies in the 1989 Finance Act. These changes will in the main affect businesses rather than the person in the street but they are an important pointer to what may happen in the future. There can be few business people who are unaware of the EC's plans for 'harmonization' by the end of 1992. VAT features as a major part of this programme and it is likely that in the foreseeable future there will be significant changes made to the structure of VAT in this country. The detail of such changes is beyond the scope of this book but it is important enough to be brought to the attention of every person involved in the running of a business whether it is large or small. All businessmen and women should keep a watchful eye on future developments.

What follows is a guide to the more common goods and services covered by the schedules for zero rating and exempt supplies. It is not an attempt to reproduce the law. Each group heading is numbered as it appears in the schedules. Examples are given of items falling within and outside each group. Zero rating also extends to items exported (see Chapter 8).

Zero rating

Group 1: Food
Most foodstuffs and the means of getting them, including plants, seeds and animals, are zero rated, with some notable exceptions. These exceptions and the problems of catering are discussed below.

Packaging and putting up for sale
Complications arise in the food trade as the liability of a product may be determined not solely because of what it is but by the way it is labelled or put up for sale. For instance, some substances such as bone meal may be zero rated as animal feeding stuffs, or standard rated as fertilizer or pet food. Butchers may sell minced offal at the zero rate unless it is labelled as pet mince. Malt extract, grains and fruits are zero rated unless sold as ingredients for home made wines and beers.

Thus liability to VAT on an item may depend on the way in which it is sold.

Fresh fruit and juices
It is, perhaps, interesting to note the relationship between food and drink. Take an orange. As a fruit you can buy it from a shop free of VAT. However the moment it is squeezed and turned into fruit juice it becomes liable to VAT at 15%. All fresh fruit juices are liable to VAT at 15% despite their obvious nutritional value.

Zero Rated	Taxable at 15%
a Food. b Mousse, general desserts. c Cakes, pastries, candied peels, biscuits. d Tea, cocoa, coffee, extracts of yeast, milk, meat. e Pork scratchings, raw nuts. f Malt extract, grains etc. not sold for making beers, wines. g Animal feeding stuffs, poultry feed. h Food plants or seed. i Edible livestock; cattle, sheep, poultry etc.	a Food additives. b Ice cream, water ices. c Chocolates, sweets, crystallized fruits, chocolate biscuits. d Fruit juices (fresh or concentrates), bottled mineral water, beers, wines and spirits. e Potato crisps and similar, salted or roasted nuts, popped corn. f Ingredients for home brewed beers, and home made wines. g Pet food, bird seed. h Ornamental plants or seed, seed growing kits. i Horses, pets, racing pigeons.

Catering

Food sold as meals in restaurants, cafes and in premises and areas without general public access, eg football grounds, is liable to VAT at 15%. Prior to 1 May 1984 food prepared for take-away consumption was zero rated. The difference between an item bearing tax and one not bearing tax depended not necessarily on the item itself but where it was sold. For example, a hot dog vendor would be liable to VAT on his sales if he set up his stall inside a footall ground but not if he sold from his stall on a street corner or in a public park.

From 1 May 1984 the law changed. Now hot food and drink sold as take-away is liable to VAT at 15%, as well as food and drink sold in restaurants and cafes. The sale of freshly baked hot pies by a baker has been held by a VAT tribunal to be the sale of hot take-away food in certain circumstances. However this decision was overruled by the High Court, which decided that the tribunal had not looked properly at the seller's purpose for heating the pies.

Cold food, eg sandwiches, milk, is still zero rated when sold as take-away. If you sell both standard and zero rated food, you will either have to keep a separate account

Zero Rated	Taxable at 15%
Cold food and drink sold as take-away, eg sandwiches, cold milk.	Items of food and drink already liable to VAT under the general regulations, eg chocolate, crisps, soft drinks, ice-cream. Hot food and drink. Food and drink sold for on-premises consumption or as catering to private functions.

of each type of sale to calculate the amount of tax you have to pay, this is called Scheme F, or use the special scheme for caterers, which is described on page 63.

Group 2: Sewerage services and water

Most sewage and water charges levied by local and water authorities are outside the scope of VAT, otherwise the disposal and treatment of sewage is zero rated. The disposal and treatment of industrial waste and farm waste is subject to VAT at 15%.

Zero Rated
a Sewage disposal and treatment, emptying of septic tanks.
b Water

Taxable at 15%
a Disposal of farm waste, cleaning and maintenance of sewers and drains.
b Distilled water.
c Bottled mineral water.

The United Kingdom has been forced to introduce legislation which will bring the treatment of sewerage and water services into line with its EC obligations. From 1 July 1990 emptying cesspools and septic tanks, etc. and the supply of water to a business which is a 'relevant industrial activity' will be subject to VAT at the standard rate. Relevant industrial activity includes a business in the water and energy supply industry, the extraction of ores and minerals, the manufacture of metals, minerals and chemicals, engineering, metal goods and motor vehicle manufacture and the construction industry. Supplies of sewerage services and water to other businesses will remain unaffected.

Group 3: Books, journals, pamphlets and newspapers

Most reading matter is zero rated from pamphlets to encyclopaedias. The zero rating extends to the cost of printing but not to the preparatory work (eg payment to authors, consultants).

Zero rating does not extend to architects' plans or engineering plans.

Zero Rated
a Books, pamphlets, newspapers, periodicals, children's picture books.
b Music sheets, maps, charts.

Taxable at 15%
a Stationery, business cards, greeting cards, calendars.
b Framed maps or charts.

Group 4: Talking books for the blind and handicapped; wireless sets for the blind

These items are zero rated when supplied to the Royal National Institute for the Blind or similar charities.

Group 6: News services

The supply of news information was zero rated until 1 April 1989. The zero rating was removed to comply with the United Kingdom's EC obligations.

Group 7: Fuel and power

All sources of domestic and commercial heat, light and power are zero rated. As with food, substances can either be zero rated or charged with tax depending on what they are sold as. For example:
a Fuel oil is zero rated unless it is sold for road fuel.
b Wood is taxable at 15% unless sold as firewood or logs for burning.

Zero Rated	Taxable at 15%
a Coal, coke, solid fuels, firelighters. b Gas and fuel oil. c Electricity, air conditioning, including charge for cold storage of goods.	a Matches. b Gas and fuel oil when sold as road fuel.

As part of the United Kingdom's EC obligations the following supplies will become subject to VAT at the standard rate on 1 July 1990:
All supplies of fuel and energy to a business user. Supplies to domestic consumers, residential homes, hospices and charities will still qualify for zero rate relief. Small deliveries of fuel will remain zero rated. Supplies to mixed premises, eg a shop with accommodation above, must be apportioned between the two rates unless at least 60% is for domestic use.

Group 8: Construction of dwellings, etc.

From 1 April 1989 the zero rate applies to supplies by builders, contractors and subcontractors in the course of construction of dwellings and certain other buildings and to the grant of a major interest in such buildings by the persons constructing them. Zero rating applies to supplies of goods and services but not professional and managerial fees.

The following buildings are zero rated:
1 buildings designed as dwellings – ie houses and flats;
2 buildings intended for use solely for a relevant residential purpose: this means use as a children's home, as a home for the elderly, disabled, people with mental disorders, or people with drug and alcohol dependency problems, as a hospice, or residential accommodation for school children, students, or members of the armed forces, as a monastery or nunnery, or as an institution which is the main residence of at least 90% of its occupants. It does not include hospitals, prisons or hotels.
3 buildings intended for use by a charity solely for a relevant charitable purpose. This means any use except in connection with any business carried on by the charity or letting the building to a third party.
4 buildings intended for use by charities as village halls and community centres providing social or recreational facilities.

Except in the case of a dwelling, a builder or contractor can only zero rate his supplies if the person to whom he makes the supply has provided him with a certificate to the effect that the building is to be used for a relevant residential purpose or a relevant charitable purpose. The certificate must take the form, shown in VAT Notice

709/2. Any person who provides such a certificate incorrectly may face a penalty equal to the tax evaded unless he has a reasonable excuse for doing so. Where there is a change in use of a zero rated residential or charitable building within ten years of its completion, or an interest in the building is granted which is exempt from VAT, the person occupying the building or who granted the exempt interest must account for VAT on the value of the part of the building which is put to a different use or over which an exempt interest has been granted (Schedule 6A)

A major interest includes the freehold sale or grant of a lease for a period greater than 21 years. In the case of a lease zero rating applies only to the lease premium, or the first rent payment if there is no premium. Zero rating does not apply to dwellings if occupation throughout the year is prevented by planning permission or restrictive covenant. The supply of a share in a time shared property cannot be zero rated.

Also zero rated is the supply of goods and services in the course of construction of a permanent park for residential caravans except where residence throughout the year is not permitted. From 1 April 1989 supplies in the course of construction of all other buildings and civil engineering works, and their freehold sale within three years of completion became subject to VAT at 15%.

Before 1 April 1989 zero rating applied to the construction and sale of all buildings irrespective of type. Transitional rules have been introduced so that where contracts and commitments were entered into before 21 June 1989 (the date of the judgment of the European Court of Justice which precipitated these changes) zero rating can still apply. The transitional rules are not set out here and anyone seeking further guidance should consult their professional advisers and their local VAT office.

Group 8A: protected buildings

From 1 April 1989 the grant of a major interest in a protected building by a person who substantially reconstructed it will only be zero rated if the building remains as or becomes a dwelling or is intended for use solely for a relevant residential purpose or a relevant charitable purpose. Similarly, approved alterations will only be zero rated in the same circumstances. A protected building is a listed building or scheduled monument. To qualify as a major reconstruction either 60% of the work carried out to the building must be in the form of approved alterations or no more than the outer walls and external features must remain. An approved alteration is normally one which has been given listed building planning consent. Before 1 April 1989 the zero rating provisions applied to all listed buildings and not just dwellings, etc. Zero rating applies to goods and services supplied in the course of construction but not professional fees.

A final word of caution; the construction industry is a complex area when it comes to VAT liability. Getting it wrong is costly both in terms of financial and tax penalties. Get professional advice if in doubt and ensure your contracts allow you to add VAT to your price if necessary.

Group 9: International services

Schedule 3 to the VAT Act 1983 lists certain services which are relevant to international transactions. These services include:

a Transfers of copyrights, patents, licences and trade marks.
b Advertising services.
c Services of consultants, engineers, lawyers, accountants, data processing, pro-

vision of information (but not if these services relate to transactions involving land).
d Agreement to refrain from any business activity or the exercise of any right mentioned in **a**.
e Banking, financial, and insurance services.
f Supply of staff.
g Hire of goods other than means of transport.
h Services rendered in procuring any service comprised in **a–g**.

Under Group 9 these services are zero rated if supplied by a person registered for VAT in the UK to a person in his business capacity (not in his private capacity) who 'belongs' in another EC country. But such services cannot be zero rated if they fall within Schedule 6 (ie they are exempt).

A person 'belongs' in a country if he has a permanent business establishment or is normally resident there. If he has an establishment in more than one country he belongs in the country where the establishment most connected with the supply in question is found.

These services may also be zero rated if supplied to a person belonging in a country outside the EC. Zero rating extends to otherwise exempt financial and insurance services provided to non-EC persons.

Group 9 also zero rates:

Supply of services relating to land outside the UK eg construction, surveying, legal services.

The hire of means of transport outside the EC.

Supply of cultural, artistic, sporting, scientific, educational or entertainment services outside the UK (eg, conferences held outside the UK).

Valuation services and work carried out on goods outside the UK.

Certain insurance services in relation to movement of passengers and goods outside the EC.

Certain financial services relating to export or movement of goods outside the EC.

Work carried out on goods temporarily imported into the UK on behalf of a person who belongs outside the UK.

Services rendered in procuring:
1 Export of goods from the UK;
2 Supply of goods or services made outside the UK. This includes services supplied in relation to the import of goods into the UK.

Again this is another complex area of VAT in which it may pay to seek expert advice if these sorts of transactions are material to your business.

Group 10: Transport

The following are zero rated:
a The supply, repair and maintenance of boats over 15 tons (not pleasure craft).
b The supply, repair and maintenance of aircraft over 8,000 kg (not pleasure craft).
c Carrying of passengers in any vehicle (land, water or air) designed or licensed to carry twelve or more people (including the driver).
d International 'through movements' of passengers and goods.
e Handling of ships, aircraft and goods at ports and airports.
f Shipping agents' fees.

Zero Rated	**Taxable at 15%**
a Hire of vehicle (twelve or more capacity) with driver. b Public transport fares. c Pleasure trips on vehicles of twelve or more capacity including charge for carrying passengers on boat fishing trips.	a Hire of vehicle (twelve or more capacity) without driver. b Taxi cab hire.* c Hire of tackle on boat fishing trips.

*Although taxi cab hire is in principle liable to VAT at 15% getting a VAT invoice from a cab driver may depend on whether or not the driver or cab company is registered for VAT.

Group 11: Caravans and houseboats

The following are zero rated:
a Mobile homes (not towable caravans).
b Houseboats.

Group 14: Medicines, aids for the handicapped

The following are zero rated:
a Supply of goods by a registered chemist to a doctor's or dentist's prescription.
b Supply of medical and mechanical aids to a handicapped person or charity for use by handicapped people.
c Supply of services of adapting, repair or maintenance or installation of goods supplied under **b**.

Group 15: Imports, exports

This zero rates the supply of goods once they are imported but before an entry is made.

Before 15 May 1987 this provision also zero rated supplies made between an office in the UK and an office abroad of the same company provided the company made no other *taxable* supplies in the UK.

This allowed branch offices of overseas traders and UK head offices of companies trading outside the UK to register and claim back input tax where they would not have otherwise been entitled to do so. Such offices may now be able to register under a different provision of the law introduced on 15 May 1987. (See Chapter 2, Other Registration Issues).

Group 16: Charities, etc.

The following are zero rated:
a Sale of donated goods by charities established for the relief of human distress or the protection of animals.
b Donation of goods to charities for sale by them.

c   The export of goods by a charity.
d   Supply of donated medical or scientific equipment to a health authority, hospital or research institute for the purposes of medical research or treatment where the goods are purchased with funds provided by a charity or from voluntary contributions.
e   Supply of goods to a charity providing medical/surgical treatment for handicapped persons.
f   Supply of advertising services to a charity, to promote its aims or appeal for funds.

Group 17: Clothing, footwear

The following are zero rated:
a   Young children's clothing and footwear (of a sort not suitable for wear by adults).
b   Industrial protective boots and helmets. The supply can only be zero rated if made to an individual and not to an employer.
c   Motorcycle crash helmets.

Customs and Excise Public Notice 714 gives guidance as to what sizes of clothing and footwear are accepted between Customs and Excise and the clothing trade as being for the normal limit for children's sizes.

Exempt supplies

Group 1: Land

Any grant of an interest in land or right over land or licence to occupy land is exempt from VAT unless it qualifies as a zero rated major interest (see zero rate construction above) or is excluded from the exemption and is thereby liable to VAT at the standard rate. The exemption covers leases, tenancies, even the right to come onto premises or property and occupy it for short periods such as a licence to put up a market stall at certain times and on certain days. It may be as little as the right to use a certain room or even a part of it for a short period in a single day.

The exclusions to the exemptions applying to land were changed from 1 April 1989 to bring into effect the decision of the European Court of Justice on 21 June as it applied to sales of land and buildings. For the position before 1 April 1989 see the previous edition of this book. Transitional provisions have been introduced so that zero rating still applies to sales of buildings under a legal or contractual obligation entered into before 21 June 1988.

The following are excluded from exemption and are therefore standard rated:
a   the freehold sale (grant of fee simple) of a new building or building under construction, other than a building which is a dwelling, or intended for use for a relevant residential purpose or relevant charitable purpose; a new building is one which is sold within three years of completion. This also applies to the first, but not subsequent, freehold sale of a building completed but not fully occupied before 1 April 1989.
b   the freehold sale (grant of fee simple) of new civil engineering works or civil engineering works under construction. A new work is one sold within three years of completion. Where a work is completed but not fully used before 1 April 1989, the first, but not subsequent, freehold sale is also liable to standard rate VAT.

c rights to take game or fish.
d supply of sleeping accommodation or rooms provided for the purpose of catering in a hotel, inn or boarding house.
e holiday accommodation in houses, flats, caravans, houseboats and tents.
f seasonal caravan pitches, tent pitches and caravan facilities.
g car parking.
h rights to fell and remove timber.
i facilities for housing or storing aircraft, ships and boats.
j the right to occupy seats and boxes at theatres, sports grounds, concert halls and other places of entertainment.
k the grant of facilities for sport or physical recreation, unless the period of use is for more than 24 hours, or a series of ten or more periods where certain other conditions are met.

Election to waive exemption (Schedule 6A)

A landlord whose property interests are exempt from VAT cannot recover VAT on his costs and he may have to pass this on to his tenants in the form of increased rents or service charges. From 1 August 1989 a landlord is able to elect to waive the exemption in respect of buildings which are not dwellings, nor intended for use for a relevant residential or relevant charitable purpose, and land on which a building is being constructed. If the landlord elects to tax he must add VAT to all rents, service charges and any subsequent leases and sales. The election will benefit the tenant who can recover VAT but not the tenant who cannot. If exercised over a building all the leases will become subject to VAT. A landlord cannot pick and choose which tenants will be charged with VAT and which will not. The election is irrevocable and so will apply to a freehold sale by the landlord and may therefore affect its market price. If made, a landlord cannot charge an additional amount in respect of VAT if the lease specifically prevents him from doing so. The landlord would be paying VAT out of his profits if he were foolish enough to make the election in these circumstances. The election should therefore be exercised with caution. It will generally bring immediate benefit only where the landlord has incurred VAT on a large capital outlay such as the purchase of a new building or refurbishment of an existing one where the capital cost cannot be recovered for some considerable time. If a landlord makes an election he must notify his VAT office within 30 days of making it. Elections made before 1 November will be effective from 1 August unless the landlord specifies a later date.

Reliefs apply so that only half the rent charged to tenants of buildings completed before 1 August 1989 and land in occupation before 1 August 1989 is subject to VAT in the year commencing 1 August 1989. The relief extends over four years for existing tenants who are charities. Tax is charged on 20% of the rent for the year 1 August 1989 to 31 July 1990, on 40% of the rent for the year to 31 July 1991, on 60% of the rent for the year to 31 July 1991, and on 80% of the rent for the year to 31 July 1992.

Self supply of buildings by developers (Schedule 6A)

From 1 August 1989 a developer is liable to account for VAT on the standard rate self supply of a building or civil engineering work which he has developed and which he either occupies for his own use when not a fully taxable person (ie is not entitled to claim all his input tax because he makes exempt supplies or has activities which are outside the scope of the tax) or in which he grants an interest which is exempt from VAT. The provisions apply if the occupation takes place or the grant is made within ten years of completion of the building or work. The provisions do not apply to buildings which are zero rated nor to buildings on which construction commenced before 1 August 1989. The value of the supply is the price paid by the developer for the land and the full cost of construction. If the value of the supply is less than £100,000 it is treated as being nil. Similar provisions apply to enlargements of existing buildings which increase the floor area by 10% or more. The value of the self supply in such cases is the increase in market value of the building resulting from the enlargement.

Group 2: Insurance

This group exempts from VAT all charges for insurance and reinsurance, including brokerage and agency fees.

Group 3: Post office services

The carrying of letters and parcels by the Post Office is exempt. Charges made by other carriers for carrying parcels, etc., are liable to VAT.

Group 4: Betting and gaming

Stake monies placed at gaming tables, with turf accountants, and money paid for lottery tickets are exempt. This group does not exempt charges made for admission to clubs, club membership fees and money placed in gaming machines, all of which are liable to VAT.

Group 5: Finance

This group exempts from VAT all charges made for financial transactions, transfers of money and arranging credit. It includes separate credit charges made by retailers to customers for goods bought on credit terms. Also included in the exemption are the proceeds from sales of stocks and shares and other securities and charges for underwriting and managing new issues of such securities.

It does not exempt charges made for debt collecting, for financial advice or for the management of the funds, or for safety deposit facilities, all of which are liable to VAT.

Group 6: Education

Education and research provided by schools, colleges and universities or by any other body otherwise than for profit is exempt. Exemption also extends to charges made by individual teachers for private tuition in academic subjects. Training or retraining for any profession, trade or employment is exempt if it is not carried out for profit, otherwise commercial and business training carried out for profit, together with recreational teaching, is liable to VAT.

Group 7: Health

This group exempts from VAT the services of, and goods supplied by, doctors, dentists, and registered medical and nursing staff. Also exempt is the provision of care in approved hospitals, nursing homes, etc. All such services are exempt whether provided for by the National Health Service or obtained privately.

Not exempted are the services of, and goods supplied by, practitioners of so-called fringe medicine, such as osteopaths, chiropractors, etc. These supplies are subject to VAT at the standard rate of 15%.

The provision of welfare services otherwise than for profit for charities and public bodies is also exempt. Welfare services include care of the sick and elderly, and spiritual welfare courses provided by religious organisations. The exemptions extend to incidental supplies of food and accommodation.

Group 8: Burial and cremation

Services given by undertakers for burials and cremations, including charges made for coffins and shrouds supplied in connection with a burial are exempt from VAT.

Not exempted are the supply of headstones, the supply of services from one undertaker to another and pet burials.

Group 9: Trade unions and professional bodies

Membership fees payable to trade unions and professional associations are exempt from VAT.

Group 10: Sports competitions

This exempts entry fees to sports competitions where either
a the entry fees are to be wholly allocated towards prizes given in the competition,
or
b where the competition is held by a non-profit making sports body.

Group 11: Works of art, etc.

This exempts the supply of works of art or scientific or historic interest to national museums, libraries and art galleries and similar bodies, or to bodies such as the National Trust, or to the State where such sales are exempt from capital taxes.

Group 12: Fund raising events by charities and other qualifying bodies

Supplies of goods and services by a charity in connection with fund raising events for charitable purposes have been exempt from VAT since 1 April 1989. The exemption also applies to certain other non-profit making organizations which raise funds for their own benefit. The exemption only applies to 'one-off' events which do not form part of a series of similar events.

CHAPTER FOUR

How the amount of VAT is calculated

Value on which tax is charged

VAT is added to the value you expect to receive for the supply of your goods and services. If you are a retailer, the VAT element will be *included* in the price charged and will have to be calculated as a tax inclusive fraction. The following example shows how this calculation is made.

Price charged = £23 *inclusive* of VAT
Tax rate = 15%

Fraction applied to sale price = $\dfrac{15}{100 + 15} = \dfrac{3}{23}$

Tax element = $\dfrac{3}{23} \times £23 = £3$

Therefore: £

VAT 3
Tax *exclusive* amount charged to customer ... 20
Total price charged £23

If you are a retailer you may sell both standard and zero rated goods. If this is the case you may have to make further special calculations to establish how much of your total sales is subject to VAT. You will need to do this before you apply the tax fraction described above. These special calculations can be made in a variety of ways and there are special rules. They are called '*Retailers' Schemes*'. Some are more complicated than others and these are discussed in Chapter 9.

Special cases

Second-hand dealers

In some cases VAT may be charged inclusively on the difference between the selling price of an item and its purchase price. This is the case for many dealers in second-hand goods. There are special rules for such persons and special accounting procedures. They are discussed in more detail in Chapter 10.

Such schemes are optional, but will usually work to your benefit. You will pay less tax. However, more paper-work is involved in maintaining the detailed records of purchases and sales required to operate the schemes.

Deposits

You do not have to account for VAT on deposits taken as security for leased or hired goods, for example. This remains the case even if the deposit is forfeited because the goods are returned damaged. The deposit represents compensation and is not the payment for a supply. You must account for VAT on deposits which are payments in advance but if the goods or services are never in fact supplied to the customer you may reclaim the VAT you have accounted for in advance. For example, a hotel will have to account for VAT on deposits taken from guests as advance payments but if the deposit is forfeited because the guest does not turn up the hotel may reclaim the VAT it has already accounted for. If the deposit is in fact described as a booking fee, administration fee or something similar the hotel is not entitled to reclaim the VAT on the payment as Customs and Excise would regard this as a supply of services.

Discounts

If you offer discounts for prompt payment, VAT is chargeable on the discounted value and not on the full value even if the discount is not earned.

If the discount relies on an event (i.e. it is a contingent discount) which may or may not occur, VAT is chargeable on the full value. The VAT may be reduced at a later date when the discount is earned, eg in the case of a discount given where a certain level of purchasing is made by the customer in a given time.

Disbursements

These are, for example, payments you make on behalf of a customer/client to a person to whom your customer/client owes money. This may be done in the course of your engagement, eg a solicitor paying a client's bills for him. VAT is not chargeable on the amount which you seek from your client by way of reimbursement. You are effectively just getting back what you have paid out as an agent. These outlays must be itemised separately on your invoice to the client. Such disbursements do not entitle an agent to reclaim any input tax on the expense as it is a supply to the client. However, if an agent does make purchases in his own name on behalf of a client, he may deduct any VAT charge on the invoice made out to him, providing he issues a corresponding VAT invoice to his client and accounts for the same amount of output tax to Customs and Excise.

Goods taken from stock for personal use

If you take goods for your own personal use on which you have claimed back input tax, you must account to Customs and Excise for VAT on the value of stock taken. The value of stock for this purpose is the purchase price paid, so the output tax owed equals the input tax claimed back.

Barter type deals

VAT is charged on the open market value of the transaction, eg the value that would be attached to the supply if if were paid for in money under normal trading conditions.

Sales between connected persons

The use of open market values may be directed by Customs and Excise if a transaction is made at less than open market value and it is between connected persons. This means, for example, husband and wife, partners and companies under common control.

A direction can be made in respect of any supply which took place within three years prior to when the direction was issued.

Postage and packing
If you supply zero rated goods and make a single charge to cover incidental packaging and postage, you have made one zero rated supply for VAT purposes. However, if you show a separate charge for packing and postage, or the packing is more than incidental, ie it has its own intrinsic value, such as a porcelain container, then the packaging or postage may become liable for VAT.

Amusement and gaming machines
Takings from amusement and gaming machines are subject to VAT. The VAT is accountable on the gross takings of the machine when it is emptied, with no deductions allowed for rental charges, profit share deductions, etc. VAT is normally payable in this way by the person supplying the facility of the machine. This may be either the occupier of the premises where the machine is situated, eg the landlord of a public house where such machines are sited, or the machine owner, depending on the agreement reached between the machine owner and the hirer.

Party plan selling
Some companies sell retail goods to customers through agents who are not registered for VAT. Customs and Excise may direct such firms to account for output tax on the price charged to customers by their agents. Such a direction may be contested where it can be shown that the 'agent' is in fact trading in his own right and is not a mere agent of the company.

Free gifts and samples
A free gift of goods by a business is a supply for VAT purposes and VAT must be accounted for to Customs and Excise on the cost of such gifts to the business unless:
a The cost of the gift does not exceed £10 (excluding VAT), and
b The gift is not one of a continuous series of gifts to the same person.
The cost of the gift is taken to be the price for it (excluding VAT) by the business.
   However if the gift is not free but sold for a nominal sum of money, eg £1, then VAT is only payable on the nominal amount paid. This provision in the law can be usefully used where, for example, you want to give away goods used in the business to your staff. If you were to give them away you would have to account for VAT at 15% of the cost of the business. (By concession, for used equipment cost is taken to mean the value you would expect to get for the used equipment if you were to sell it). If, instead of giving the equipment away, you agree to sell it to an employee for £1, then you only have to account for VAT as $\frac{3}{23} \times £1$.
   Beware, if the person you wish to sell the equipment to is a connected person, Customs and Excise could direct you to substitute open market value for the £1 you have calculated VAT on at any time up to 3 years after the event. An employee is not usually a connected person, unless he or she is either a relative of the proprietor(s) or a controlling director of a company (see above).
   A free gift of services is not generally a supply for VAT purposes. VAT need not be accounted for on free trade samples of industrial goods.

Mixed supplies
Sometimes you may want to put a single price on a supply of mixed goods which are liable to different rates of tax, ie part standard rated and part zero rated. The charge you make may be apportioned on the basis of either cost or open market value and VAT accounted for on the standard rated portion.

eg You charge a customer £100 inclusive of VAT for a mixed supply of goods. The standard rated goods cost you £30 inclusive of VAT. The zero rated goods cost you £40. You may calculate VAT as

$$\frac{3}{23} \times \frac{30}{70} \times £100 = £5.59$$

This amount of VAT should be clearly shown on any invoice you issue.

You may substitute VAT exclusive figures to calculate VAT at 15% of the result. You may also substitute open market values in place of costs.

There is no compulsion to use either cost or open market values in preference to the other in any given situation, as long as the method chosen gives a fair and reasonable result. If your product is new on the market, you may find it difficult to use the open market value method unless you know of a similar product you can make a direct comparison with.

Mixed supplies must not be confused with composite supplies, where in reality only one supply is being made. For example, a laundry service is a single supply of laundry services and cannot be broken down into its constituents, eg soap powder, water, electricity. Mixed supplies refer to separately identifiable products sold together, eg story books and cassette recordings.

Hotels, inns and guest houses

If the stay of a guest lasts for four weeks and more, irrespective of week-end breaks or whether the customer stays in the same room VAT is charged on a reduced amount after the fourth week. For example, a hotel charge may effectively consist of a charge for accommodation, facilities (eg room service, TV, etc.) and meals.

VAT must be accounted for on:

a Full value on meals.
b Full value of other incidentals, eg bar charges.
c The value of facilities which are included in the charge for accommodation. Facilities must be valued for VAT purposes as at least 20% of the inclusive charge for accommodation.

Two types of situation may arise after the fourth week:

i   You reduce your total charge to the customer by the reduced VAT.
ii You maintain the same total charge to the customer. In doing so you actually charge more VAT to your customer than in **i** above. You also receive more income for yourself than in **i** above. However, the calculations necessary are much more difficult to understand.

Given a case where you normally charge £100 plus £15 VAT ie £115 all in for board and lodging, opposite are two examples of how you calculate the reduced VAT in cases **i** and **ii** above.

Example 1: As in 'i' above

Description	Excluding VAT	VAT
Total charge for full board	┌── 100	
Meals element (realistically assessed).	├── 20 × 15%	3
Total charge less meals element (ie accommodation and facilities).	└── 80	
Value of facilities – 20% (this must be valued as 'at least' 20% of the value of accommodation and facilities).	16 × 15%	2.40
Totals	↳ 100	5.40

Therefore your charge to the customer after four weeks is:
£100 plus £5.40 VAT for full board.
If you have VAT 'inclusive' charges here, you will have to calculate the VAT 'exclusive' amounts by using the 'VAT fraction' (see page 29).

Example 2: As in 'ii' above

Description	Including VAT	Excluding VAT	VAT
Total charge for full board	┌── 115		
Meals element (realistically assessed).	├── 23	20	3 (a)*
Total charge less meals element (ie accommodation and facilities).	└── 92	89.32	2.68(b)*
Totals	↳ 115	109.32	5.68

* (a) See page 29 (VAT fractions)
* (b) To obtain this: $\frac{3}{103}$ × 92. The fraction is $\frac{3}{103}$ when the VAT rate is 15%. If the rate alters ask your VAT office for the new fraction.

Therefore your charge to the customer remains at £115 after four weeks. (£109.32 plus £5.68 VAT).

Rooms let out in a hotel other than for the accommodation of guests and for catering purposes are exempt from VAT rather than standard rated. For example, rooms let out by a hotel in which a conference or meeting is held, areas let out to shops are exempt from VAT. The law changed from 1 November 1986 and prior to this, virtually all space let out inside a hotel was subject to VAT at 15% and eligible for the value reductions described above if let out for more than 28 days.

CHAPTER FIVE

Issuing invoices

Tax invoices

The rules governing the issue of tax invoices are rather complex and there are many confusing overlaps. There are five different sorts of tax invoice which may be issued, namely:

a   Full tax invoices.
b   Less Detailed tax invoices.
c   Modified tax invoices.
d   Petrol and Diesel tax invoices.
e   Cash and Carry wholesale tax invoices.

The detail demanded for each type of invoice is different and the essential requirements are summarised by the table opposite.

The general rule is that if you are registered for VAT you must issue full tax invoices, if the customer is also registered for VAT. This general rule is, however, relaxed considerably in certain instances. If you are a retailer or similar trader, there is a simplification of this general rule. It is that you need only issue a tax invoice if requested by the customer. Also, even if the customer does so request, the full details need not be given if the value of the sale is £50 or less (including VAT). This is called a Less Detailed invoice. Generally speaking these invoices should not record several sales at multiple rates. Suitably amended credit card slips will be sufficient under this heading, e.g. VISA, ACCESS etc.

Even if the amount is for more than £50 you need not give full details if you are:

a   Selling petrol and diesel fuel.
b   Selling as a cash and carry wholesaler.

This is because there are special provisions for simplified invoices in such cases.

Further to the above rules, if you are a retailer, you can issue what is called a modified tax invoice. But this can only be used if the customer agrees to it.

Use the above information to decide what categories you fall into and then refer to the following table to see what detail has to be included on the invoice(s) that apply.

Using a broad, common sense approach, it can be seen that the idea behind these confusing rules, is to provide not only a check on your own VAT calculation charges but also a means to ensure that a VAT registered customer has evidence of his purchase, from which Customs and Excise can verify his claim for input tax.

Full tax invoices must not be issued for items sold under the second hand goods schemes (see Chapter 10). Tax invoices need not be issued for zero-rated sales.

Self billing

Some registered persons need not issue tax invoices at all, eg in 'self-billing' situations. This is where customers make out their own invoices for supplies from VAT registered suppliers. The supplier must agree to the use of self-billing by his customer and refrain from issuing invoices in such instances. Customs and Excise must approve such a scheme and will state any conditions to which it is subject. It is the responsibility of the person using the self-billing scheme to check that his suppliers are registered for VAT throughout the period of use of the scheme. If a supplier deregisters from VAT without the scheme user's knowledge, the scheme user will continue to self-bill VAT when it is no longer legally due. The scheme user will not be legally entitled to reclaim the 'VAT' charged as input tax and may have difficulty in recovering it from his supplier. Self-billing arrangements should therefore be approached with caution. After 28 July 1988 Customs and Excise may claim money due in respect of VAT understated on a self-billed invoice from the person using the scheme rather than the supplier.

Table of invoice requirements

Full tax invoice	Less detailed tax invoice
a Invoice number. b Date/tax point (see page 37) c Your name and address. d Your VAT registration number. e Customer's name and address. f Description of supply with analysis of sales at different VAT rates. g Amount charged excluding VAT. h VAT charged. i Discounts.	a Your name and address. b Your VAT registration number. c Date/tax point (see page 37) d Description of goods. e The gross amount charged. including VAT. The VAT rate that applies to the sale.

Modified tax invoice
The requirements are the same as for full tax invoices except:
  i For each positive rate supply the VAT inclusive value need only be shown.
  ii At the bottom of the invoice separate *totals* must be shown for
   a The total VAT charged.
   b The VAT exclusive total of positive rated supplies.
   c The VAT inclusive total of positive rated supplies.
   d Zero rate supplies.
   e Exempt supplies.

Petrol and derv tax invoices	Cash and carry wholesaler sales
The requirements are the same as for full tax invoices, except: a The vehicle registration number can be put instead of the customer's name and address. b The type of supply and number of gallons sold need not be shown.	Modified till roll slips will do here, but they must contain: a Suitable 2 or 3 digit coding for each class of goods. A decoding list must be distributed to each VAT registered customer. b If an item costs over £50 it must be *separately* coded, or identified in writing on the invoice.

Business gifts

You must account for VAT on a business gift which costs you more than £10 or which is one of a series given to the same person. You must not issue a VAT invoice for gifts. However, if he is entitled to claim the VAT back on the item, the recipient may be given a 'tax certificate'. Although such a certificate does not bear the legal status of a

VAT invoice, it does contain all the same basic details and for all practical purposes constitutes the same thing. It must be headed 'Tax Certificate', and clearly state that no payment is necessary and that output tax has been accounted for on it.

Credit notes

If you issue a credit note, eg because a customer returns foods for which he has already been invoiced, then you must include this on your VAT return in order to reduce the amount of VAT due. This will be done by clearly adjusting your records and accounts to reduce the sales value and VAT by the amounts on credit notes issued in any period. Credit notes should be sufficiently detailed (similar to full tax invoices) and identify the original invoices and the reason for the credit.

Sales by bailiffs or similar persons.

Such sales are considered for VAT purposes to be made by the VAT registered person whose items are being sold. They are taken to be sales in the course of his business with VAT being accountable on them where appropriate. The auctioneer's sale document to the buyer will be treated like a VAT invoice.

Computer invoicing

This is standard practice for many invoice issuers. The tax invoice detail requirements still apply as above. If you intend to use such a system you must give one month's notice to your local VAT office, you have the right to impose conditions on its use and check its operation from time to time.

CHAPTER SIX

When is VAT due?

Tax points

There is a point in time when a supply takes place for VAT purposes and the VAT on the supply must be recorded in the accounts even though it may not be paid until the return has to be submitted. The date a supply takes place for VAT purposes is called the *tax point*. Tax point rules become especially important when there is a change in the rate of VAT.

If you are a retailer using the standard method of reckoning gross takings (see page 46) there are rarely any technical problems over tax points as supplies take place when you receive payment.

However, if you issue invoices you must have special regard to certain tax point rules.

The basic rule is that a tax point occurs when goods are taken by the recipient, or made available to him. If the supply is a service, it is the date when the service is performed and completed, unless the service is a continuous one (eg, a lease) where payments are made every so often. If this is the case the tax point becomes the date when each payment is received or an invoice issued, whichever is the earlier.

These basic rules do not usually apply for most registered traders issuing invoices. This is because if you issue an invoice within 14 days of the basic tax point, then the invoice date becomes the actual tax point.

Invoice issuers may also apply to their local VAT office for an extension of the 14 day rule. This is rarely refused if the extension is for a reasonable period, eg one month, and is required to fit in with your normal accounting procedures, eg month end billing.

Therefore, if you issue an invoice in accordance with the above rule on 30 June and your VAT return is for the period from 1 April to 30 June, you will have to pay the VAT charge on that invoice, even if you have not yet received the money from the customer. On the other hand if you allow a customer to take goods on 31 March but invoice on 14 April, you will account for the tax on the goods in the return period to 30 June and not 31 March.

If a customer never pays for goods and services you have invoiced, you may be able to claim relief from the VAT you will have paid to Customs and Excise (see Chapter 7).

Cash accounting

From 1 October 1987 taxpayers with a turnover of less than £250,000 pa were given the option of accounting for VAT on a cash basis. Obviously in this situation the normal tax point rules will not apply. See Chapter 14 'Records and Accounts' for a more detailed explanation of the cash accounting system.

Deposits

If a deposit is effectively an advance payment on account, the normal tax point rules apply.

However, if it is the nature of a refundable payment as security, its receipt does not create a tax point.

Sale or return

If you supply goods in this fashion, a tax point generally arises when 'adoption' takes place, eg a sale whereby the right to return the goods is given up by the customer, or 12 months after the goods are made available to your customer, whichever is sooner.

Personal consumption

Goods taken for your own use have their tax point when they are removed from stock, or put aside for your use.

CHAPTER SEVEN

When the debtor does not pay

The general rule is that VAT is payable on all supplies you make in the course of your business, irrespective of whether you receive payment or not from your customer (although most retailers and those using the cash accounting system will not be in this position – see Chapter 14).

However, relief from VAT paid to Customs and Excise but not received from the customer may be reclaimed in certain circumstances.

Bad debt relief

This is an important provision. It applies to debts owed by persons who become formally insolvent after 1 October 1978, and not to those becoming insolvent before that date.

You must be able to show that the person who owes the money to you is 'formally insolvent'.

This is a special term and one of two conditions must be met for it to apply. Either:

a   the debtor must be declared bankrupt by a court, or have entered into a scheme approved under the Insolvency Act 1985, eg where the debtor enters into a scheme of arrangement for the benefit of his creditors.

b   if the debtor is a limited company, the court must have ordered its winding up, or there must be a creditor's winding up. From 1 April 1986 a company becomes insolvent if a person appointed to act as the company's administrator or administrative receiver issues a certificate to the effect that, in his opinion, if the company were to go into liquidation it would not be able to meet the debts of unsecured non-preferential creditors. The administrator is required to give notice of his issuing such a certificate to all the company's unsecured creditors.

You must put in a claim against your debtor for the VAT exclusive amount that you are owed. This is because the VAT element is to be claimed from Customs and Excise. Make sure you keep a copy of this as proof of the claim.

You must obtain a written statement, which acknowledges the claim from the receiver or liquidator acting on the insolvency.

Ownership of goods must have passed to your customer. You must be able to show from your records that you have charged VAT to the debtor, accounted for it, and paid it to Customs and Excise.

If you reserve title to the goods you supply until payment for them is received, you must formally give up your rights to the goods if you wish to take advantage of the bad debt relief. You can do this either by sending a written statement to this effect to the person in charge of the insolvency, or by including such a statement with your claim. You should weigh up which alternative is commercially more desirable; giving up title to your goods or foregoing the bad debt VAT relief. If your title is not sound you may be better off claiming the relief. If in doubt seek legal advice.

If you receive a part payment of the debt from the customer, you can only reclaim VAT on the unpaid amount. This is straightforward if you can allocate the payment to a particular supply you made (eg £100 plus £15 VAT invoiced; £57.50 received. £115 − £57.50 = £57.50 still owed, ie £50.00 plus £7.50 VAT − refer to VAT fraction page 29).

However, if this cannot be done, eg if you have a running account with a customer, then you must allocate payments received to the earliest supplies you made. You then claim bad debt relief for the VAT on unpaid amounts. In such a case, you may have to apportion VAT on a supply for which you have effectively received a part payment under this rule. An example may best illustrate:

Supply No.	Date of Supply	Excluding VAT (£)	VAT (£)	Including VAT (£)
1	1.10.83	100	Zero rate	100
2	1.11.83	200	30	230
3	1.12.83	300	45	345
	FORMAL INSOLVENCY			

You receive £250.00 before insolvency. This is allocated to supply 1 (£100) leaving £150 to be allocated to supply 2. This leaves a bad debt of £80.00 remaining on supply 2 (£150–£230). This is nothing left to be set off against supply number 3, so the £45.00 VAT on this may be reclaimed in full as bad debt relief.

We must apportion VAT on supply 2 to calculate how much may be claimed as bad debt relief.

$$\frac{\text{Bad debt remaining}}{\text{VAT inclusive total on supply}} = \frac{80}{230} \times 30 \text{ (VAT on supply 2)}.$$

$$= £10.43 \text{ VAT bad debt relief on supply 2.}$$

Therefore total VAT relief = £45.00 (supply 3) plus £10.43 (supply 2) = £55.43.

A number of supplies made on the same day constitute *one* supply for VAT bad debt relief purposes.

Mutual debts

You may owe your customer some money which is less than his debt to you. In such a case, bad debt relief can only be claimed by applying the VAT fraction (page 29) to the VAT inclusive balance he owes you.

How to claim relief

The VAT reclaimable is entered in your VAT return (see Chapter 14).

CHAPTER EIGHT

Exporting goods and services

Export of goods

Goods exported from the United Kingdom (the UK) (other than those sent to the Isle of Man) are free from VAT. They are classed as zero rated sales. This may include supplies to foreign going craft, provided that proof of official orders for tax free supplies is obtained from the master of the ship or aircraft. Also a declaration must be obtained that the goods are only for use on a particular craft which is entitled to zero rated stores. The supply must be made direct by you to the craft, or via freight forwarders.

The person who may claim the zero rating is the final exporter, ie the one who is actually involved in the exportation (although you may still claim zero rating if the goods are put through an auctioneer, sold through an export house, or if you supply certain goods to overseas visitors in the UK (see page 42).

Therefore, just because goods are supplied to someone who will use them and eventually export a product he makes for them, does not mean that the supplier of such goods can also zero rate them.

However, there is an exception to this where goods are supplied to 'another business in the U.K.' for processing before being exported. Here you must consider whether you are simply supplying what are virtually raw materials for use in manufacture of something else, or whether you are supplying something which will be merely processed in some way before export. If the latter is the case you may zero rate your sale, but you can only do so if you do certain things, of which the following are most important:

a You must keep a log of all such sales. This must contain a record of the purchaser's name and address, invoice details, and description of goods. Proof and date of export must also be kept (see **b** below). This log is additional to the normal VAT sales records.

b The goods must be exported within six months of sale to the processor. Proof of this fact must be obtained from the exporter (processor) within one month of the actual exportation that he makes.

It is only then that you can enter the sale in your VAT sales record as a zero rated sale. (This is an exception to the usual tax point rules, see Chapter 6.)

c The goods sold to the processor must not be used in any way other than for processing, as explained above.

Goods exported direct by the supplier are zero rated. But if no evidence of export is obtained within three months of the export, VAT must be paid on the sale. This would be calculated on a tax inclusive basis. For example, if the sale price is £230 the VAT (if the tax rate is 15% on the goods) is

$$\frac{15}{115} \times £230 = £30$$

41

Sales to overseas visitors

These sales may be zero rated if certain conditions are met. There are two different sets of rules for the zero rating of goods supplied to overseas visitors in the UK. Which rules you apply depends essentially on whether the sale is of smaller goods (being those which can be carried with your personal baggage) or of larger goods. We shall deal below with larger goods. Small goods are reviewed under the heading—*Personal Export Schemes* (see page 43).

Larger goods

The following conditions must be met if the sale is to be zero rated:

a Zero rating can only apply when evidence of actual export (ie removal of the goods from the UK) is received.

So, if you sell goods to an overseas visitor in this country who is going to take them out of the UK, you must arrange for him to send evidence of the export back to you when he leaves the UK. This evidence must be received back within one month of the export.

b The goods themselves must be exported within three months of the sale.

So, you must have the whole thing completed—exports and documents, within four months of the actual sale, for the sale to be zero rated.

c You must keep a record of some evidence to show that the customer was 'an overseas visitor'. To do this you need to show that he was not a UK resident (eg take his passport details).

d You must keep evidence to show that the customer intended to leave the UK within three months of the sale (eg a signed declaration by him).

e When you actually make the sale, an entry must be recorded in a log. This is separate from the normal VAT sales records. Then, when the export evidence is

Checklist of proof of exports

Mode of export	Type of proof necessary for zero rating
SEA	Bill of Lading Certificate of Shipment from the shipping company.
AIR	Air Way-Bill signed by the airline company, with details of date, flight, etc.
VEHICLE ON FERRY	The driver should inform the ferry company of the goods being exported and obtain an appropriate Bill of Lading or Certificate of Shipment.
POST	Evidence of posting should be obtained, eg correspondence on the sale, copy invoice, freight details, evidence of payment and receipt of it.

This checklist of requirements is for VAT purposes only. Remember, Customs may require other documents when you export.

received back from the customer, you may enter the sale as zero rated in your VAT sales records.

If the larger item is a boat bought by an overseas visitor to sail abroad, zero rating may be claimed, subject to the conditions a to e on previous page. The supplier must also ensure that the overseas customer complies with any general Customs requirements regarding his departure.

Repairs

Repairs to temporarily imported boats and motor vehicles may be zero rated. This includes the sale of any parts used, as long as the sales invoice analyses them separately.

Personal export schemes

There are two schemes which allow retailers to sell goods free of VAT to foreign visitors and also to UK residents going abroad for more than one year. The schemes are not compulsory, and whether you use them or not depends on how much you value the goodwill of your foreign customers. The schemes do not apply to the following goods:

a   New and used motorcars.
b   Boats.
c   Direct export of goods.
d   Goods personally exported for business purposes (eg merchandise and samples).

Provisions are made for zero rating these goods under the general arrangements for exports.

Retail exports

Retailers and others may zero rate goods sold personally to

a   Community travellers, ie a member of an EC State (other than the UK) who is visiting the UK and returning to another EC country.
b   Overseas visitors, ie anyone else visiting the UK who is leaving to go abroad and has not been in the UK for more than 365 days in total in the last two years.

Goods sold to Community travellers must be above certain minimum values to qualify for zero rating. The values are:

a   Over £55, if the destination is Eire.
b   Over £200, if the destination is Denmark and Greece.
c   Over £250, if the destination is any other EC country.

What the seller must do

a   Ask the customer for proof of entitlement, eg passport or ID card.
b   Charge the customer VAT and tell him this will be refunded on return of form VAT 407, duly authorised.
c   Complete VAT 407 with the customer's help. Attach copy invoices to the form.

What the customer must do.

a   Community travellers—produce goods and hand VAT 407 to Customs for authorisation at country of destination. Return authorised form to seller.

b Overseas visitors—produce goods and hand VAT 407 to UK Customs at the port of departure. Return authorised form to seller.

Goods must be exported within three months of sale. If evidence of export is not received within four months of sale, the seller must account for VAT in his records.

Alternative evidence of export is acceptable if VAT 407 is not produced or authorised, eg import duty receipt, evidence signed by Customs/Police/Notary Public. From 1 April 1988 a fully detailed invoice can be used in place of Customs and Excise forms 407 and 435 to prove that goods have been exported.

Sales to crews of foreign vessels and to UK residents leaving for overseas

To qualify for this scheme, crew members must either be 'Community' travellers, overseas visitors or UK residents leaving for more than twelve months. Other UK residents also qualify for this scheme if leaving for more than twelve months.

The goods cannot be given personally to the customer. They must be forwarded direct to the ship or craft on which he is leaving, either by the seller or by a forwarding agent.

The same minimum value limits apply to goods sold to persons leaving for EC countries as those which apply under the retail export scheme.

For persons going to EC countries, form VAT 435 must be completed with the customer's help, and produced to Customs at the port of final destination. The form must be returned to the seller properly authorised, otherwise VAT may have to be accounted for on the transaction.

For persons going to non EC countries, form VAT 435 must be completed and attached to the goods being exported. These should be sent to the shipping company with instructions to produce them to UK Customs before the customer's departure. The shipping company should return the form, properly authorised, to the seller.

Forms

Ask your local VAT office for a stock of forms (VAT 407 and VAT 435) appropriate to your requirements.

Export of services

There is no blanket provision for zero rating the export of services as there is for goods. Certain international services may be zero rated. These are contained in Group 9 of the Zero Rate Schedule explained on page 23.

CHAPTER NINE

Special schemes for retailers

Retail schemes

If a business issues tax invoices to its customers for sales and supplies, the business will have a record of all the VAT charged to customers in any period (output tax).

However, if you are a retailer, you will be taking money for the sale of goods or services without issuing tax invoices for every sale. You then have to calculate the amount of VAT that is included in your 'takings' (sales). You will not add VAT on top of the actual takings as your customers will have been charged this in the inclusive price. Therefore you would not take 15% of the takings when calculating VAT. If you do, you will be overpaying tax.

Special calculations must be made to extract the VAT from the takings. Also there are further complications if some of your takings are at more than one rate of tax. How do you separate them if you have just one till for all sales in which there are sales at different rates of VAT?

This is what retail schemes are all about. There are essentially nine different schemes and they are identified by letters of the alphabet—A B C D E F G H and J. There are further adaptations to some of these which vary some of the basic scheme provisions. These variations have been introduced to make the schemes more fair to certain users and more widely available. In general, however, the adaptations create more work for the user.

Retail schemes can only be used to calculate VAT due on retail supplies. The definition of a retail sale is not always as straightforward as you would think. If you have any doubts at all as to the status of your supplies and eligibility to use a retail scheme, discuss the position first with your local VAT office. Before October 1987 some non-retailers were allowed to use retail schemes. There have been special changes over concessions to users to allow for change in accounts systems.

Most retailers using these schemes are shopkeepers, but they need not be. Just because you are a retailer does not mean that you need never issue tax invoices. You must, if requested by another registered person (see Chapter 5).

Businesses that have retail outlets, but are not otherwise retailers, may use the schemes for these outlets provided that completely separate accounts are kept for them. Otherwise they are restricted to the schemes A and F (see pages 47–8).

Retailers and their takings

Before going into the mechanical detail of the schemes themselves we must discuss your records of *gross takings*.

A record of takings should be kept daily. The records should be of your *gross* sales for each day's business. This means everything taken for sales transacted in the day. This is a very generalised statement, and it must be expanded. We shall do so at some length as it is important.

There are two ways of arriving at your gross takings, namely
a The standard method.
b The optional method.

As a general rule you cannot change your chosen method of calculating gross takings. Most retailers use the standard method. This is usually both the easiest and the most advantageous (for instance you will not at any stage account for VAT on bad debts). However, it may posibly conflict with the accounts required for income tax purposes, so do inform your accountant of the method you choose for VAT purposes.

The standard method
The standard method of recording gross takings merely records the takings actually received on each day.

Things to be included in your record of gross takings	Things to be excluded from your records of gross takings
Amounts received from Customers. Cost (including VAT) of goods you've taken for personal use.	Deposits received (this does not mean a first instalment on a purchase or rental agreement).
Takings via Credit Cards, eg Access, Visa, Luncheon Vouchers.	Refunds of money given for things returned by customers.
Copy Vouchers, eg where you accept a price reduction coupon which entitles you to a reimbursement from the supplier.	Payments received for exempt supplies.

The optional method
The optional method of reckoning gross takings accounts for the full value of goods sold on the date a sale is actually made, not when the cash is received from the customer.

For example on 1 February goods are sold to a customer, on credit, for £20. The customer pays on 1 March.

Under the standard method of recording gross takings, £20 is accounted for on 1 March when the customer pays.

Under the optional method £20 is shown in the takings on 1 February when the sale is actually made.

Few retailers actually operate this optional method.

Customs and Excise say you have not declared all your takings
Many retailers have received an assessment for underpayment of VAT, on the basis that gross takings have not been fully disclosed. There are many ways in which Customs and Excise attempt to prove and calculate the amount of under-declared VAT (see Chapter 17).

Different schemes

We are now ready to look at the different methods of calculating the tax on your sales by using the special schemes. As we have said there are nine basic schemes and a number of adaptations but you may not be able to use some of them because of:

a   the size of your business, ie by virtue of its turnover.
b   the fact that takings may include takings from a service you have sold.
c   the takings represent the sale of goods you have manufactured.
d   you sell goods and services at different rates of VAT.

So, before we go into the details of how to operate each scheme, we list in the table below those schemes you are prevented from using if you fall into any of the above categories. This means that you can dismiss certain schemes right away, without having to read through them all.

Scheme	Turnover requirements	How many rates of tax can be coped with	Service or manufacturing element allowed or not
A	None	One	Allowed
B	None	Two	Allowed if it is charged at the higher rate
B1	None	Two	Allowed if it is charged at the higher rate
B2	Under £500,000 per annum	Two	Allowed if it is charged at the higher rate
C	Under £90,000 per annum	Two or more	Not allowed
D	Under £500,000 per annum	Two or more	Not allowed
E	None	Two or more	Not allowed
E1	None	Two or more	Not allowed
F	None	Two or more	Allowed
G	None	Two or more	Not allowed
H	None	Two or more	Not allowed
J	None	Two or more	Not allowed

Unless you use scheme F or A, your takings must not include sales of *assets*, but VAT must be charged on those sales if the transaction is subject to VAT. In these cases, calculate the VAT separately on such sales and enter a separate record of them in your accounts. If you use Scheme B you may also include sales of assets, provided they are at the standard rate of VAT.

Some of these schemes involve much more accounting work than others, and these are usually designed for the larger traders. However, the choice is yours. We provide the table overleaf as a guide to the scheme, or schemes, which may be suitable for your business.

We shall deal with the different schemes in order of similarity and complexity.

Scheme A

This scheme is designed for retailers whose takings are all at one rate of VAT.

So we are here faced with a record of gross takings for the period, and have to

Scheme	Generally suited more to small/medium sized retailers	Generally suited to large retailers
A	*	*
B	*	
B1	This one sits on the borderline of both	
B2	*	
C	*	
D	*	
E	*	
E1		*
F	*	*
G	This one sits on the borderline of both	
H		*
J		*

extract the VAT. To extract the VAT due on your sales you multiply your gross takings by what is called a *VAT fraction*.

You arrive at this fraction by the following formula:

$$\frac{\text{Rate of tax}}{100 + \text{Rate of tax}}$$

Therefore, if your gross takings are £2,300 for the period, and the VAT rate is 15%, the formula becomes:

$$= \frac{15}{100 + 15} \times £2,300 = \frac{3}{23} \times £2,300$$

Therefore your tax on sales (output tax) is £300.

Scheme F

This scheme is for those retailers who can analyse their takings according to the different rates of VAT they bear when they make the sale. This may be done, for example, by:

a A coded till where each sale is entered on a till roll with a code by the side of it to illustrate the rate of VAT at which the sale is liable. You must, however, make sure you press the right code button for each sale.

or

b By having separate tills for takings at different VAT rates.

So at the end of the period you will have records showing sales at different rates of VAT. You must then apply the VAT fraction(s) (see Scheme A above) to these figures to calculate the VAT due on the sales (output tax).

If you press the wrong key on the cash till, or put money in the wrong till you may underpay or overpay VAT. Where an underpayment arises it may be picked up by the

Customs and Excise when they inspect your accounts, and the extra tax demanded from you. If you find yourself in this situation see Chapter 17 for advice.

Scheme D

General

This is a popular scheme for those retailers with sales at different rates of VAT who do not wish to have separate or analysed tills to record takings at the different rates, but are prepared to spend some time analysing their purchases records. Bear in mind the turnover limit of £500,000 on this scheme.

Mechanics

Broadly speaking, the scheme works by apportioning your takings for the period to get the amounts chargeable to VAT at different rates. To this you then apply the VAT fraction (see Scheme A above) to extract the VAT on your sales (output tax).

The proportion is based on your purchases of stock at different rates, to your total purchases of stock. These figures must include the VAT you've paid to your suppliers as shown on their invoices. The VAT you pay on assets and items not for resale is reclaimable by you as input tax in the usual way, but these purchases play no part in your scheme calculations.

So, if we assume there are just two rates of VAT in force, a standard rate of 15% and a zero rate; the output tax will be established by applying the following example.

The proportion

Case facts

		£
a	Purchases in tax period, including VAT, for resale at 15% rate =	500
b	Purchases in tax period for resale at zero rate =	1,000
c	Therefore total purchases, including VAT, for resale =	1,500

Calculating the proportion

$$\frac{a \text{ Purchases in tax period including VAT for resale at 15\%}}{c \text{ Total purchases for resale in tax period including VAT}} = \frac{£500}{£1,500}$$

This must then be applied to your gross takings for the period to get the takings calculated to be liable to 15% VAT.

So, if your takings are £3,000:

$$\frac{500}{1,500} \times £3,000 = £1,000$$

You have now calculated that £1,000 of your takings are inclusive of 15% VAT and therefore the balance of £2,000 is zero rated.

All you now have to do is to calculate the VAT included in this £1,000. For this purpose you apply the VAT fraction for 15%, which is

$$\frac{3}{23} \times £1,000 = £130.43$$

Do not take 15% of £1,000 as you will pay too much tax.

Unfortunately this is not the end of the story. You also have to make an *annual adjustment*. This involves:

a Adding up all your takings figures for the last VAT year.

b Adding up all your purchases for resale that you have used in your calculations for the last VAT year.
c Making one big calculation in the same way as usual, except that you calculate output tax for the whole year.
d Comparing the output tax figure for the year's calculation with the total of the output tax already calculated over the year for each quarter.
e Entering any difference—which may be extra tax due from you or to be repaid to you—on your VAT return when you are making the adjustment. This will be the return for the fourth quarter in the year (see Chapter 14 on how to complete VAT returns).

These adjustments rarely make any great difference, and many people forget to do them. However, you are still obliged to make the adjustment.

You must also make such adjustments if:
a The VAT rate changes.
b You stop using this scheme altogether.

Suggested accounts format for Scheme D

				Purchases of goods for resale			Purchases not for resale	
Date	Invoice	Supplier	Total charged	Amount charged at 15% excluding VAT	VAT charged	Zero rated	Amount excluding VAT	VAT

The columns for PURCHASES OF GOODS FOR RESALE can be extended to cope with any new rates of VAT which may be brought in. Records like this combine details of all the VAT you can claim back. If you wish, you can extend the analysis into different sorts of purchases and/or columns for details of your payments, eg date/cash/cheque.

Commentary

You may overpay or underpay VAT using this scheme if your profit margins vary considerably on standard and zero rate goods. The scheme does not account for stock fluctuations. This may also produce distortions. For example, if your mark-up is higher on average for zero rated goods than standard rate goods, you may pay more VAT using this scheme than under another scheme.

Scheme C

General

This scheme does not rely on your gross takings, although you still have to keep a record of them.

Broadly speaking it adds on a percentage to your purchases for resale which bear VAT, to arrive at an estimated figure for sales subject to VAT. Then you apply the VAT fraction to extract the VAT.

Mechanics

This scheme is designed for small retailers with an annual turnover of less than £90,000. It is easy to administer and the books you need to keep are comparatively very simple. The percentage you have to use is set by the Customs and Excise and varies depending on what your business is (see table on page 53).

You may pay more or less tax than you would if you used a more accurate scheme. This will depend on whether your profit margins are higher or lower overall than the one built into scheme C.

There are ways of checking to see if it is likely that you are paying too much tax or not and the work involved may be well worth it, if the result shows that the scheme operates against you.

You can get a very rough idea of your actual average profit mark up by taking your most popular item sold and calculating the margin on that.

Mark ups are calculated like this:

Cost per item including VAT = 10p
Your selling price per item, including VAT = 12p
Therefore gross profit = 2p
Therefore mark up percentage = $\frac{2}{10}$ = 20%

However, if the Customs and Excise rules for scheme C say you must use 50% due to the nature of your business then obviously you ought to think very carefully before deciding to use scheme C.

The 20% mark up on one item does not end the story. You could sell some highly-priced items at very low mark ups, eg 2% and this would mean your average mark up was really less than 20%.

The likely situation is that you will have many different mark ups on different items.

A 'straight average' (eg $2 + 8 + 17 \div 3p = 9$), would be insufficient as a means of gauging your actual average mark up because you may buy more of some items than others—all with different mark ups. There is a quite simple test you can do to arrive at a realistic mark up which you could say reasonably applied to all your purchases in the course of a year. There are four stages:

a Choose your most popular items bearing VAT that you sell and calculate their profit mark up as already explained.

b Choose an average trading period, eg one spanning three months. Add up all the amounts bought of the different items you have chosen in **a** separately.

c Multiply the amounts in **b** by the mark up each item has. Then add all these amounts.

d Divide the total in **c** by the sum of all the purchases you've made of the items for the period.

The best way of doing this is by setting up a table. If the instructions above have not been immediately clear to you, then just follow the routine used in the table below, eg we shall take just two items so as to make the calculations clear.

Item	Mark up calculated (X)	Purchases in period (Y)	(X) × (Y)
A	20	50	1,000
B	5	100	500
Totals		150	1,500

To get your average weighted mark up:

$$1,500 \div 150 = 10\%$$

Notice the difference here with a 'straight average' of $20 + 5 \div 2 = 12\frac{1}{2}\%$.

So if the scheme C table below says you have to use 20% then you can feel reasonably confident that to use scheme C will mean paying more than is truly due. In such a case you are advised to read on and consider the alternative schemes that are available.

Using the scheme

If you are a jeweller with purchases of stock in a VAT period of

	£
VAT exclusive cost	4,000
+ 15% VAT	600
Total cost	4,600

you mark-up £4,600 by 75% (extracted from the table) to get your estimated sales figure:

	£
$4,600 \times \dfrac{75}{100} = £3,450$	4,600
	3,450
Therefore total sales estimate =	£8,050

Therefore total sales estimate

To calculate the VAT in £8,050 you apply the VAT fraction (see page 29). Therefore tax on your estimated sales (output tax) will be.

$$8,050 \times \frac{3}{23} = £1,050$$

Sort of business	Customs and Excise classification	Mark up to be used (%)
Off-licences	8207	$15\frac{1}{2}$
Confectioners/Tobacconists/Newsagents	8214	$15\frac{1}{2}$
Grocers	8201	20
Dairymen	8202	20
Butchers	8203	20
Fishmongers	8204	20
Bakers	8206	20
Greengrocers/Fruiterers	8205	40
Radio/Electrical retailers	8222	40
Bicycle/Pram shops	8225	40
Bookshops/Stationers	8226	50
Chemists/Photographic shops	8227	40
Music shops	8232	50
Department stores	8211	50
Variety and general stores	8212	50
General mail order houses	8213	70
Footwear shops	8215	60
Mens/boys wear shops	8216	50
Womens/girls wear, household, textiles, general clothes	8217	50
Retail furriers	8218	60
Domestic furniture, floorings/Upholsterers	8219	50
Antique dealers, second-hand furniture, art dealers/stamps	8221	50
Radio and TV rental shops	8223	50
Hardware, china and wallpaper shops	8224	50
Opticians	8228	50
Leather goods, sports goods, toys and fancy goods	8231	50
Florists/nurserymen and garden shops	8233	60
Pets and pet food shops	8234	50
Other shops (not food shops)	8239	50
Jewellers	8229	75
Health and wholefood shops	–	50

Suggested accounts to keep
The scheme records that are recommended are the same as for scheme D (see page 49).

Commentary on scheme C
Be wary of using scheme C. In addition to remarks already made on mark ups the following criticisms are relevant:

a The scheme assumes that you sell everything you buy in a period, and that there are no fluctuations in the value of your stocks over a period of time. If you have more value tied up in stock at the end of a period than at the beginning, you will effectively have paid tax on the increase, even though it has not been sold (this is because you have uplifted to the selling price all purchases and calculated the tax due on this figure).

b Even if you think that your actual average mark up is about that demanded by scheme C, you may find that you end up by making less actual profits than you originally thought, due to losses (eg theft of stock, spoiled stock, big discounts, etc.)

Scheme B

General
For this scheme you need a record of your gross takings, and a record of your purchases for resale at their different rates of VAT. The idea is to estimate the selling price of your lower rated purchases of goods for resale and deduct this from your takings figure for the period. This leaves a figure for takings that beat VAT. Currently the zero rate will be the lowest rate.

Mechanics
The uplifted figure (ie your estimate of the lower rate sales must take into account things like special offers, etc. You can arrive at the estimated sales figure by various means.

For instance you can establish an average mark up percentage to apply to each class of your lower rate purchases, eg all vegetables, all breads, all biscuits, etc. You then apply this class mark up to purchases of the items to arrive at their sales figures.

Suggested accounts format for scheme B:

Date	Invoice number	Supplier	Amount excluding VAT	VAT	Amount on invoice at the lower rate of VAT	Estimated selling price of lower rate purchases

(Refer to scheme C above for an example of how to calculate fair mark-up percentages.) At the end of the tax period the total of all the estimated sales figures will be deducted from your recorded gross takings to leave the takings figure subject to VAT at 15%. To calculate the VAT you then apply the VAT fraction to this figure, ie $\frac{3}{23}$ (Chapter 4).

A further requirement to use this scheme is that the zero rated sales must be 50% or less of the total Customs and Excise inclusive turnover over the course of the year.

Commentary on Scheme B

If you are a small/medium sized retailer who is eligible to use scheme B, it is worth considering that scheme. It is easy to operate and quite effective.

However, there are certain features you ought to be aware of. The scheme does not account for any increases or decreases in the stocks over a period of time. If your lower rate goods undergo stock increases of some size, you will underpay VAT because you would not have sold items, but you would have assumed them sold, and deducted them from your takings, to get the apportionment of sales for VAT.

If there was a stock decrease in lower rated sales you would overpay VAT.

Scheme B1

Scheme B1 is an adaptation of scheme B. The scheme helps overcome some of the potential disadvantages of using scheme B. As we have seen above, large zero rate stock fluctuations may distort the results of scheme calculations. This may result in under or over declared output tax.

Scheme B1 compensates for the effects of these stock movements. The scheme provides for an annual adjustment which uses the scheme figures for the whole year making an allowance for stock increases or decreases. Stock values are taken as the expected selling prices. The opening zero rate stock value at the start of the year is added to the expected zero rate sales value of goods acquired during the year. The closing zero rate stock value at the end of the year is then deducted. The adjusted result gives a more accurate assessment of actual zero rate sales throughout the year. This in turn gives a more accurate assessment of standard rate sales made in the year when the calculated zero rate sales are deducted from the recorded gross takings.

Commentary on scheme B1

The smaller retailer may find the detailed annual stocktaking requirement of the scheme too much to cope with. However, for the retailer who already compiles reasonably detailed end of year stock figures it may not be too difficult to analyse the zero rate stocks from the others. Similarly you may not find the scheme too difficult if your zero rate stock holding is small.

Scheme B2

Scheme B2 offers an easier method of calculating output tax.

One of the practical difficulties with the scheme B method of calculation is the problem of ascertaining the class mark up. Class mark ups have to be applied to the various classes of zero rate purchases to arrive at zero rate sales for scheme calculations. You have to decide which items to put into a class and then how to work out a fair and average mark up. To avoid these difficulties in the scheme Customs and Excise have established a number of class mark ups that can be used by small retailers under the adapted scheme.

Small retailers for this purpose are those with an annual turnover of less than £500,000. Otherwise the calculations are the same as for scheme B.

The mark ups are:

Food	20%
Children's clothing	35%
Books, maps, etc.	40%
Newspapers, magazines, etc.	33%
Other goods	15%

Commentary on scheme B2

Scheme B2 is a simple adaptation of scheme B that is available to small retailers with a mixture of standard and zero rated sales. If you are serious about using scheme B2 you ought to check that the fixed mark up used by the scheme is about right for your type of zero rate stock lines. A good way of calculating this is to use the example given in scheme C earlier this chapter.

Scheme E

General

This is a scheme that does not rely on your gross takings to calculate the VAT due on your sales. However, you still have to keep a record of them.

It is not one of the more difficult schemes to operate. Basically it works by using your estimated sales figure for standard rate sales. The difficult part of the scheme is establishing the figure for the selling price and ensuring that in doing so you do not act to your disadvantage. The estimated selling price must include VAT and so must the purchase price that you mark up to obtain that estimate.

Mechanics

You will have to calculate your sales at the standard rate by estimating what your customers will pay for the goods you have bought. This means taking account of any factors such as special offers, discounts, etc.

You will have to satisfy Customs and Excise when they come to inspect your accounts that your calculations are properly based. Perhaps the most effective way of establishing sales at standard rate is to keep a record of goods purchased uplifted to a selling price by using mark up percentages for different goods or *classes* of goods. For example, sell for 40p and buy for 30p, mark up is:

$$\frac{(40p - 30p)}{30p} \times 100\% = 33\%$$

Therefore add $\frac{1}{3}$ to the purchase price of those items.

If you decide to use a mark up average for classes of goods, and not individual items, you must take great care in establishing your average mark up. A straight average may not be good enough. For example, if you sell three different sorts of sweets with mark ups of 10%, 20% and 30% the straight average you could calculate as applying to all purchases of sweets would be 60% ÷ 3 = 20% However, most of your turnover in sweets could be sweets with only 10% mark up and very few at 30%. Therefore if you use 20% mark up on all sweet purchases, you may pay too much VAT. There is a way you can 'weight' your average to get a fairer one. This method is described in the section on scheme C (see above).

This may seem like a lot of work, but if you are serious about using this scheme, it may prove worth it in the long run. Of course, if you uplift each line of goods in our example; at 10%, 20% and 30% mark up for sweets individually, the result will be more accurate. This method is, however, very time consuming.

The value of initial stocks must also be analysed into goods at different rates, and the selling price worked out as discussed above. VAT will be payable on these. The stock-take need not be one of pinpoint accuracy, but it must be 'reasonable'. Otherwise the sales value of the goods received for resale in the three months before starting the scheme may be used.

When you have uplifted the sales figures, you must apply the relevant tax fraction to calculate the VAT due inside the estimated sales figure. For example, with a 15% VAT standard rate the fraction is:

$$\frac{15}{15 + 100} = \frac{3}{23}$$

There is quite a good check you can apply to see if the scheme is working reasonably accurately or not. You are estimating your standard rate sales and keeping a record of your actual sales. The difference represents your zero rate sales. Compare these zero rate sales with zero rate purchases in the period (adjusted for stock variations, etc.) to see if the mark-up percentage is what you would expect on your zero rated goods. (A method for showing you what you should expect is shown on page 52.) If it is not you could be paying more or less tax. The problem could lie with your standard rate mark-up.

If a change in tax rate occurs you must use another tax fraction from the date of change. Also you must have a stocktake at the date of change and establish the selling price of goods held including VAT,

a At the old rate of VAT; and,

b At the new rate of VAT.

The new stock figure will be used in your VAT calculation at the new rate of tax. To **a** you must apply the old VAT fraction. The result is a *tax credit* for you, which must be entered on your VAT 100 in box 5 (see Chapter 15). This is because you will have already paid VAT at the old rate on stocks held when the rate changed.

Suggested accounts format for scheme E

Below is an example for two rates of tax, normally a standard rate of 15% and a zero rate. It can be extended if new rates are introduced.

Date	Supplier	Invoice number	Amount excluding VAT	VAT	Amount excluding VAT	VAT	Expected price of goods 15%	Expected selling price of goods at zero rate VAT

The two VAT columns will give you total tax on purchases that you can claim back as input tax. Extra columns can be made up if multiple rates are introduced.

Commentary on scheme E

This scheme does not take into account *stock fluctuations*. If you have a very large build up in the value of stocks that bear VAT you could be *uplifting* the purchases of those stocks and therefore paying VAT on them, although you will not have sold the goods. Obviously, it depends on how long you keep the extra stock, and the value involved, but in inflationary times this could affect cash flow and certainly result in a loss of interest at the bank, etc. For small businesses it could be insignificant.

The danger of average 'class' mark ups has been explained and you are advised to consider this before deciding to use the scheme. Also, if you do decide on scheme E, consider regular reviews.

Scheme E1

Scheme E1 was designed to compensate for distortions to scheme E style calculations that are created by stock increases and decreases in a period.

Scheme E1 is a much more complicated scheme because of its additional book-keeping requirements. The scheme accurately calculates the VAT due on sales by working out the standard rate sales in a period from the actual quantities sold of standard rate lines of goods. The quantity of each stock line purchased in a period is adjusted for opening and closing stock quantities. The result represents the quantities of each stock line sold in the VAT period. This quantity is then marked up to its actual gross sales value to give the sales subject to VAT in the period.

Commentary on scheme E1

The scheme is an accurate way of calculating VAT due. It is, however, costly in terms of administrative time and effort. It will not generally be suitable for smaller retailers.

Scheme G

General

This scheme is one of the more complicated ones. It is similar to scheme D which has already been described earlier in this chapter. You can use the same records that are suggested for scheme D.

Mechanics

Scheme G works by making an analysis of your purchases of stock at different rates of VAT, and calculating the proportion of purchases at different rates in relation to the gross purchases of stock. You then apply these proportions to your gross takings for the period. The result represents your sales subject to VAT. The next step is to apply the appropriate VAT fraction to extract the VAT out of the sales. For a standard rate of 15% this is $\frac{3}{23}$.

The scheme then requires that $\frac{1}{8}$ is added to the VAT you have calculated. The result is the VAT due on your sales (output tax).

The main difficulty with this scheme is the manner in which you must arrive at the percentage of purchases for different rates of VAT.

The basic idea is that one whole year's purchases figures are used all the time to arrive at the percentages to apply to your sales for each VAT quarter. Obviously when you start using scheme G you may not have a whole year's analysed purchases records from which to calculate percentages for a whole year (ie the current quarter's figures, plus the previous three quarters). So there are different rules for quarters 1 to 3 and quarter 4 onwards. It is probably best, therefore, that we look at these situations separately.

Quarters 1 to 3

1st Quarter: For the first quarter you must include the stocks you hold in your initial calculations. However, valuation of stocks need only be a reasonable estimate.

Your proportion is arrived at by taking your purchases of stock at different VAT rates in the quarter, adding the initial stock figure to it and comparing this figure to the total purchases for resale. For example:

Total stock held	£1,000
Stock held at 15% VAT	£500
Purchases in period at 15% VAT	£3,000
Purchases in period at zero rate	£1,000
Total purchase for resale	£4,000

All figures must include VAT.

So your proportion for this first quarter of using the scheme would be:

$$\frac{\text{Purchases at 15\% in period + stock chargeable at 15\%}}{\text{Total purchases for resale in period + total stock}} = \frac{3{,}000 + 500}{4{,}000 + 1{,}000} = \frac{7}{10}$$

this proportion would then be applied to your gross takings for the period to arrive at a figure for your sales at 15% VAT.

So, if gross takings in the period were £10,000 the amount of takings subject to VAT at 15% would be

$$\frac{7}{10} \times £10{,}000 = £7{,}000.$$

We must then apply $\frac{3}{23}$ to extract the VAT = £913 output tax.

Unfortunately it does not stop here. You must then add the additional $\frac{1}{8}$.

$$913 + (913 \times \tfrac{1}{8}) = 913 + 114 = £1{,}027.$$

2nd Quarter: You will now have to use the purchases and stock figure for quarter 1, plus the purchases figure for the current (2nd) quarter to get your proportion.

eg Purchases in quarter 2 at 15% (including VAT)	= 4,000
Purchases in quarter 2 at zero rate	= 1,500
Total purchases for resale	= 5,500

Your proportion is therefore:

$$\frac{\text{Purchases + stock at 15\% in quarter 1 + purchases at 15\% n quarter 2}}{\text{Total stock in quarter 1 + total purchases for resale in quarters 1 and 2}}$$

$$= \frac{3{,}000 + 500 + 4{,}000}{4{,}000 + 1{,}000 + 5{,}500} = \frac{7{,}500}{10{,}500} = \frac{5}{7}$$

Again this will be multiplied by the gross takings for the period (quarter 2) to get your estimate of sales at 15% and then the VAT fraction plus $\frac{1}{8}$ applied to get the output tax.

3rd Quarter: The same principle applies as for the 2nd quarter but you add the figures for quarters 1 and 2 to those for quarter 3.

Quarter 4 onwards

When you come to this quarter, you use the figures for it and the previous 3 quarters, but you do not include the quarter 1 stock figures. Otherwise the same principles apply.

Do note that no annual adjustments are necessary as they are with scheme D. This is because a four quarterly running total is used, or initially quarters 1, 2, and 3 plus stock, which makes the proportions effectively self-adjusting.

Recommended accounts
As per scheme D (see page 49).

Commentary on scheme G
As you will have seen, there is quite a lot of work involved in the administration of scheme G. The $\frac{1}{8}$ addition to output tax can make a considerable difference, to the extent that the results may be unfair to you, and it may pay you to consider alternative schemes (possibly even coded tills and scheme F (see page 48)).

There exist the following pitfalls with scheme G:

a If you buy comparatively expensive, positive rated stock which does not sell, you will pay tax on a higher percentage than is truly reflected in your standard rated taxable sales. So you may pay too much tax.

b Any large standard rated stock build up is not accounted for in the scheme, which will lead to the same effect as in **a** above.

Scheme H

General
This again is a more complex scheme which will take up more administrative time and effort. It is claimed to be a more accurate method than many other schemes (apart from those that analyse sales when the sale actually takes place, eg schemes A and F). However, you must weigh up the time involved in keeping the accounts for this scheme, against the possible benefits of the increased accuracy achieved from using it.

Mechanics
This scheme shares the same basic principles as scheme G. You are therefore asked to read the following differences that scheme H has from scheme G, and then read scheme G with this in mind.

Suggested accounts format for scheme H

Date	Invoice number	Supplier	Amount excluding VAT	VAT	Expected selling price of standard rated purchases for resale including VAT	Expected selling price of zero rated purchases for resale

You can use these purchases records for all purchase entries, but do not use the uplift columns for things bought otherwise than for resale, ie assets. They do not form part of the scheme calculations, but the input tax is reclaimable by you in the usual way.

The figures for stock and purchases in scheme G are the projected sale values for scheme H, ie you have to use the expected selling price of your stock held and purchases of stock. Your records must show how you have uplifted your stock and purchases to get a fair estimate of what you expect it will sell for. You may know precisely what the sale price will be or you may apply an average mark up percentage for the class of goods the item falls into, eg biscuits, clothes, etc. (See scheme C above). If on starting to use scheme H you do not have an accurate stock record you can use the value of goods received for the previous three months.

Effectively, each purchase invoice must be entered in your accounts with the items on it split into different sums according to the rates of VAT they bear. Then you must uplift these sums to get the figure that customers will pay.

Whereas in scheme G you have to add $\frac{1}{8}$ to your final calculated figure of tax due on sales (output tax), you do not do this in scheme H.

Commentary on scheme H

Scheme H can be turned to your advantage to check whether your recorded takings for any period are reasonably correct.

You will have a record of your expected sales (takings) from your purchases records for scheme H. If you adjust this for stock variations (increase or decrease in value), by adding your opening stocks valued at their expected selling price and deducting your closing stocks values at their expected selling price, you should have a figure very close to your recorded gross takings. This assumes your estimated sales figures for scheme H are reasonably correct. There may exist inaccuracies due to subsequent events, eg higher and unexpected wastage (spoiled goods). However, if there is no reason for a large difference, you ought possibly to think along the lines that there may have been theft of stock, or money from the till.

Also, Customs and Excise may use this method to verify your records of gross takings. If there is a large discrepancy they may rely on this as evidence to assess you for extra tax on the difference. If this happens to you see Chapter 16 for advice.

Scheme J

General

This scheme is in many ways like scheme H. It works by calculating the proportion of your expected sales at the standard rate. The records you need to keep are really the same as for scheme H. Again, this is a difficult scheme, and requires a lot of work to administer. It may possibly be more accurate than some retail schemes but this must be weighed against the extra work involved. Essentially this is a scheme designed with larger retailers in mind.

Mechanics

You will form the proportion using:

a The selling price that is expected to be realised on goods for resale held at the beginning of your VAT year, ie opening stocks. This will have to be analysed into goods held at the different rates of VAT.
b The selling price that is expected to be realised on goods you buy from the beginning of your VAT year to date, ie to the end of the tax period you are working on. Again this will have to be done for all goods bought at different rates of VAT and the selling prices obtained by uplifting purchases for resale to their selling price in your records.

If you cannot do this exactly for each item you may use an average class mark-up percentage which, when applied to the purchase, will give its estimated sale price. (See scheme C above.)

So, by using the figures in **a** and **b** above, you get the following information, if there are only two rates of VAT in force, namely a standard rate of 15% and a zero rate.

i   Selling price (including VAT) of goods in stock at the beginning of the year subject to VAT, at 15%.
ii Selling price (including VAT) of goods in stock at the beginning of the year at the zero rate.
iii Selling price (including VAT) of goods purchased to date at 15% VAT.
iv Selling price of goods purchased to date at zero rate.

The proportion used in the calculations is taken for the whole VAT year, i.e. 4 quarters + stock at the beginning of that year. The proportion will be:

$$\frac{(i) + (iii)}{(i) + (ii) + (iii) + (iv)}$$

In other words

$$\frac{\text{Selling price of 15\% initial stocks + purchases to date}}{\text{Selling price of total stocks and total purchases to date}}$$

This proportion is then multiplied by your gross takings for the quarter for which you are completing a VAT return. The result gives you your standard rate (15%) sales included in your gross takings. To this you will have to apply the appropriate VAT fraction. For 15% this fraction is:

$$\frac{15}{15 + 100} = \frac{3}{23}$$

Unfortunately this is not the end of the story. At the end of your VAT year you will also have to make an annual adjustment.

The annual adjustment is made by calculating a new proportion which must be applied to your gross takings for the whole of your VAT year. This will give you an adjusted figure for your gross takings subject to VAT for the whole year. You will then have to apply the VAT fraction to get the revised annual output tax. This adjusted figure is then compared with the output tax you have calculated individually for each quarter in the year. The difference will show either extra tax to pay, or tax to be repaid to you. The adjustment is entered in the appropriate box on the VAT return (see Chapter 14 for completion of form VAT 100).

We must now look at this new proportion mentioned above, ie the annual adjustment, and how to arrive at it:

It is calculated by taking the proportion figures as usual for the 4th quarter but you now deduct from these the closing stock, figures at the end of the VAT year, valued at their selling price to customers, including VAT, where applicable. So you will need records of closing stocks held at the different rates of VAT.

The fourth quarter's ratio will read: (assuming two rates of tax, a 15% standard rate and a zero rate):

$$\frac{\text{Selling price of 15\% initial stock and purchases to date} - \text{selling price of closing stock at 15\%}}{\text{Selling price of total initial stocks and total purchases to date} - \text{selling price of total closing stock}}$$

There are specific provisions in scheme J for certain variations to suit some business peculiarities. For example, opening stock and closing stock are used in the calculations on a quarterly basis as you go along rather than waiting for an annual adjustment. This attempts to ensure a fair adjustment to account for any stock fluctuations.

However, if your stocks vary in respect of the rate at which they sell and are held, you may pay much more or less than you should. Naturally you would be more concerned over the former. To take an example: You sell goods at the 15% rate and the zero rate. The zero rate stocks you hold are very few compared with standard rate stocks, although zero rate sales are high. In this situation your percentage will be 'top heavy' because there is little value in opening stocks at zero rate compared with those at 15%. Therefore, you will end up paying more tax than is fair until the end of year adjustment. So you may lose interest at the bank, etc. It may also cause cash flow problems. With a large business these considerations are very important.

When these problems arise there can be some variations to scheme J. You should write to your local office in the first instance. Typical variations that Customs and Excise will consider are:

a *Quarterly* stock adjustments instead of annual ones.

or

b Leaving out opening stock from your calculations until the fourth (last) quarter in your VAT year when you carry out the annual adjustment. In this last quarter you would then take into account opening *and* closing stocks.

Recommended accounts
These are as for scheme H.

Retrospective retail scheme changes for small traders
A recent development of benefit to the smaller business has been the introduction of a scheme whereunder a newly registered business may change from one retail scheme to another 'retrospectively', for any period up to the date of its first VAT visit (normally within 18 months of registration).

Furthermore, other traders with an annual turnover of less than £120,000 will be allowed to apply to their local VAT office to change retail schemes 'at any time' with retrospective calculations of VAT due up to 3 years.

Refunds are only permitted where the VAT difference is greater, on average, than £50 per annum.

Caterers

Caterers may have sales at the standard or zero rate. Food eaten *on the premises* as in the case of a cafe or restaurant, for example, always bears standard rate VAT. Some *take away* foods are zero rated. These are restricted to *cold food and drink* such as milk and sandwiches sold for consumption off the premises. *Hot food and drink* taken away is standard rated. Before May 1984 all take away food was zero rated irrespective of whether it was hot or cold. Some items of food sold are subject to VAT whether sold for consumption on or off the premises, eg chocolate, crisps, soft drinks.

Caterers are now involved in the difficult practical situation of how to separate their sales into the different categories for standard and zero rating.

For those who are unable to split their gross takings between the two rates by using an appropriate retail scheme such as F (see earlier in this chapter), Customs and Excise allow caterers to estimate the percentage of their takings which is liable to VAT at 15% or zero rated, whichever is the easiest. The estimation must be based on actual records kept for a representative period, and must take into account changes in trading patterns over the year.

If you decide to use this scheme you must obtain agreement from your local VAT office. If you are taking over an established business you may be able to base your estimate on the previous owner's experience.

Once your estimate is agreed you apply the percentage to your gross takings for each quarter or VAT return period and apply the VAT fraction ($\frac{3}{23}$) to the standard rated portion of your takings.

For example:

Agreed estimate of zero rated sales	20%
Gross takings for quarter	£10,000
Zero rated sales for quarter (£10,000 × 20%)	£2,000
Sales inc. VAT at 15% (£10,000 − £2,000)	£8,000

VAT due = $\frac{3}{23}$ × 8,000 = £1,043

Once such an arrangement has been approved by Customs and Excise it may hold valid indefinitely, provided that the trading pattern remains the same. A tribunal has rejected an attempt by Customs and Excise to impose a higher percentage than that originally agreed with a trader. Two days' observation of business activity by VAT officers was held not to be the best judgement the Commissioners of Customs and Excise could make.

Pharmacists

Pharmacists sell prescribed drugs which are zero rated under the present law, but such prescriptions are often made up from materials on which the pharmacist has been charged VAT. Output tax that is calculated by any retail scheme other than schemes A or F will result in too much tax being paid to Customs and Excise. To offset this they have agreed the use of a special scheme for pharmacists using schemes other than A or F.

Mechanics

For each VAT period:

a   Calculate your output tax as laid down by the retail scheme. Your gross takings should include zero rate prescription charges and NHS payments.

b   Add up all payments received in the period for zero rated medical goods and services.

c   Estimate the percentage of **b** made up from standard rate goods (agree this percentage with your local VAT office).

d   Multiply **c** by the VAT fraction $\frac{3}{23}$ (and increase by $\frac{1}{8}$ if using retail scheme G).

e   Take **d** from **a**. This is your output tax for the period.

Comments

The scheme is cumbersome and compounds any inaccuracies inherent in the retail schemes themselves. You need to record your receipts for zero rated medical supplies separately for this scheme, so with little more effort scheme F could be used for a more accurate result.

CHAPTER TEN

Special schemes for the sale of second-hand goods

Second-hand goods
There is no overall exemption from VAT for goods merely because they are being sold second-hand or in a used condition. Neither is a person exempt from VAT registration because he deals in second-hand goods. Thus all sales of used goods, equipment and machinery are subject to VAT at the normal rate. A person opening up a second-hand shop will have to register for VAT if his total turnover exceeds, or is expected to exceed, the current limit for VAT registration. There are some ways of reducing total liability for VAT which are discussed at the end of this chapter.

However, certain used goods may be sold under special schemes devised by Customs and Excise which provide for VAT to be calculated on a reduced value. To be able to use these schemes, you must be prepared to keep the very detailed records which are required by Customs and Excise. The goods which can be sold under these schemes are:

a Used motor cars (not vans or commercial vehicles).*
b Antiques, second-hand works of art and scientific collections.
c Second-hand caravans and motor cycles.
d Second-hand boats and outboard motors.
e Used aircraft.
f Second-hand electric organs.
g Used firearms supplied by licensed dealers.
h Ponies and horses.

For all these goods VAT is calculated as a part of the margin of sale price for each item, that is, the difference between the price you paid for the item when you bought it and the price you sold it for. VAT is taken to be included in the margin of sale and is calculated as a fraction of it in the same way that retailers calculate VAT included in their takings. The formula is:

$$\frac{\text{tax rate}}{100 + \text{tax rate}} \times \text{Margin of sale.}$$

This fraction is currently

$$\frac{15}{100 + 15} = \frac{15}{115} = \frac{3}{23}$$

---

* Vehicles not eligible for the second-hand car schemes are: London taxis, Land-Rovers (van types and 12-seat types), ambulances, lorries, buses. Three-wheeled cars can be sold under this scheme.

To calculate the VAT on an item which cost £300 and was sold for £369 proceed as follows:

Selling margin, £369 − £300 = £69.

VAT included in the margin $\frac{3}{23} \times £69 = £9$

VAT due to Customs and Excise on this transaction = £9.

If you are considering registration for VAT, remember it is the gross value of your sales which is counted as turnover, not merely the total margins of your sales.

Requirements of the schemes

In order to sell goods under the second-hand schemes, certain specific conditions are laid down.

a The item must have been purchased from a person not registered for VAT, or from a registered person who sold the item to you through the second-hand scheme.

b The item must not have been sold to you on a tax invoice showing VAT separately (this follows from **a**).

c You must not claim any input tax deduction on the purchase of the item.

d When you sell the item you must not issue an ordinary tax invoice for the sale but the special kind of invoice described below.

You may often find yourself purchasing items of stock from people who are either not registered for VAT, or selling items privately. You will not be able to obtain an adequate purchase invoice for such transactions. In such cases you must prepare your own purchase invoice. This must show:

i Identifying number of the invoice;
ii Seller's name and address;
iii Date of transaction;
iv Your name and address as the buyer;
v Description of the item(s) and any identifying numbers (such as registration numbers in the case of cars);
vi Gross price paid for the item(s).

The seller must sign and date the invoice to certify that the details regarding his name and address are correct.

When selling an item under the scheme you must issue a sales invoice with the same information as given in **i** to **vi**. Except in this instance you are the seller at **ii** and your customer is the purchaser at **iv**.

You must also make sure you certify the invoice with the following words 'Input tax has not been and will not be claimed by me in respect of the goods sold on this invoice'. You must sign and date the certificate.

Under each scheme a stock book must be maintained recording the purchase and sale of each item of stock. Each item of stock must be entered in the stock book on the date of purchase and it must be given a stock number.

The stock record can be regarded as being split into three areas of information.

a Details of purchase, seller and identification of goods bought.
b Details of sale and buyer of the goods.
c Accounts, stating purchase price, sale price, sales margin and tax due to Customs and Excise.

(A) Example of stock book for second-hand cars

PURCHASED

Stock No.	Date	Invoice No.	From	Reg. No.	Make Model, Year
HJ 1112	1.3.83	P.887	M. Jones 10 New St. Anywhere.	AAA 666 S	Ford Cortina 1978

SOLD

Date	Invoice No.	To:	PURCHASE PRICE	SELLING PRICE	MARGIN FOR VAT £
1.4.83	S.10001	A. Smith, 99 Old St., Anytown.	£1,670	£1,900	£230.00

ACCOUNTS

END OF VAT QUARTER TOTALS

(B) BROUGHT FORWARD UNSOLD FROM PREVIOUS VAT QUARTER

Stock No.	Date	Invoice No.	From	Reg. No.	Make Model, Year
HJ 779					
HJ 884					
HJ 996					

SOLD

Date	Invoice No.	To:	PURCHASE PRICE	SELLING PRICE	MARGIN FOR VAT £
			£900		
			£1,050		
			£1,300		

(A) = Typical stock book entry for purchase and sale details of a used car.
(B) = Summary of unsold stock brought forward from previous VAT quarter accounts

Example of used car sale or purchase invoice

HONEST JOHN'S MOTOR COMPANY, 111, Fore Street, Anytown. (Proprietor: H. John, Esq.)	USED CAR SALE/ PURCHASE INVOICE NUMBER: S. 10001 Date: 1–4–87

SELLER   H.J. Motors,
               111, Fore Street,
               Anytown.
 	
SIGNED:
 	
DATE: 1–4–87
	BUYER A. Smith,
	               99 Old Street,
	               Anytown.
	
	SIGNED:
	
	DATE: 1–4–87

VEHICLE

Make	Ford	Model	Cortina 1600 L.
Registration	AAA 666 S	Year	1979
Colour			

	£	£
SALE PRICE		1,900.00
Less Discount %		
Stock Book Selling Value		
Deduct:		
Part Exchange on Vehicle No.		
Deposit paid.		
Add:		
Road Tax		
Insurance		
Balance owing		
Cash paid/cheque/H.P.		

"Input tax has not been and will not be claimed by me in respect of the car sold on this invoice."

SIGNED   H. John   DATE   1.4.1987

An example of a stock book applicable to used cars is given on the previous page. For cars, motor cycles, boats, aircraft, etc., registration numbers, engine numbers and similar information must be recorded. For items such as antiques, works of art and scientific collections, a description sufficient to identify the goods will be all that is needed.

For accounting purposes it is recommended to rule off your stock book at the end of each VAT period, then add up the sales margins for all items of stock sold in that quarter. Multiply the total by $\frac{3}{23}$ to arrive at VAT owed to Customs and Excise for stock sold in the period. Enter this output tax in box 1 of your VAT return.

Make a brief summary of all stock remaining unsold, eg by reference to stock number and purchase price only. Carry this summary forward to the records for the next VAT period and begin again.

In this way you need never look at a record for more than one VAT period to see what stock remains unsold.

When entering values of second-hand goods on your VAT return, always enter the full value of the goods (excluding any VAT) for both sales and purchases. Do not enter just the value of the margin for tax purposes.

Other second-hand dealers

How to reduce your VAT burden

If you sell second-hand goods which are not covered by any of the special schemes, then normally you would have to account for VAT on the full price of anything you sell, where your turnover exceeds £23,600 per annum. If you buy your stock from the general public then you have no input tax to offset against the output tax you owe Customs and Excise. This puts you at a disadvantage compared with other tradespeople. There is, however, one way in which you can reduce your liability to pay VAT.

Instead of buying goods outright from people, you can act as an agent in the sale of their own goods. You will then have to account for VAT only on the commission you make. For example:

In a normal transaction:
   You buy goods from A: Price: £20.
   You sell those goods to B: Price £30.
   You pay VAT ($\frac{3}{23}$ × £30) = £3.91

As an agent:
   You accept goods from A: Retail value £30
   You agree with A to sell goods for £30 and take commission of £10 (equivalent to the profit in the above transaction).
   You sell goods to B   £30.
   You pay A   £20.
   You take commission   £10.
   You pay VAT on commission only of ($\frac{3}{23}$ × £10) = £1.30.

You will have to keep a record of the items you are selling in this fashion, who you are selling them for, and how much commission you are making on each transaction. You would need this to keep your own records straight and to produce the record for inspection by any VAT inspector who might call to examine your accounts.

Naturally most people bringing in goods to a second-hand dealer expect to receive cash straight away. There is no reason why they should not and yet still agree for you to act as their agent. You would be able to loan any customer a sum of money up to the retail value of the goods, less your commission. When the goods are sold this automatically cancels the loan.

Selling goods this way not only reduces the amount of VAT you pay. It also reduces your turnover for VAT purposes.

Say, for example, the gross value of the goods you sell in any year is £50,000. If you trade in the normal way, buying goods from people and selling those goods, you would have to register for VAT and pay output tax of £6,521 (£50,000 × $\frac{3}{23}$). If, however, you act as an agent and, say, you work on a rate of commission of $\frac{1}{3}$ of selling price, then your turnover for VAT purposes would only be £16,666 (£50,000 × $\frac{1}{3}$). You would, therefore, not have to register for VAT in the first instance.

It must be borne in mind that the ownership of goods sold in this way would never pass to the shopkeeper or dealer acting as an agent. The person who brought in the goods would have a legal right to reclaim them at any time up to the time when they are sold.

CHAPTER ELEVEN

Claiming back VAT

Inputs and input tax

Introduction
The word 'input' is used simply to describe any purchase of goods or services that a business or business person may make. Input tax is the amount of VAT that has been charged on the value of those goods or services bought.

This chapter deals with the rules that determine how much VAT can be reclaimed by a business. It is assumed for this purpose that all the supplies you make to your customers are taxable at either the positive rate or the zero rate. If you make exempt supplies there are further considerations which are outlined in Chapter 12.

Business and non-business
Generally, purchases of goods and services fall under two headings; business and non-business. Business inputs cover all purchases of goods and services which are made for the purposes of carrying on normal business activities, eg purchase of plant and machinery, stock-in-trade, overheads and expenses. The tax on such expenditure can be reclaimed from Customs and Excise with certain notable exceptions. These exceptions are referred to as non-deductible inputs and they are described later in this chapter.

VAT on purchases of goods and services which are not for the purpose of carrying on normal business activities is not input tax and cannot be reclaimed from Customs and Excise. For example, the sole proprietor who treats himself to a new colour television set, buying it through his business bank account, cannot rightly claim that it was a business input. Tax on such items cannot be reclaimed from Customs and Excise.

Some purchases may be made which cover both business and personal (or non-business) use. For instance, a sole proprietor may have a telephone on which he makes both business and private calls. In these circumstances the VAT charged on telephone calls must be fairly apportioned between business and non-business use and only the business part of it may be reclaimed as input tax.

You will probably be in a similar situation yourself. If you are, there are no fixed rules to apply. You must make your own estimation of what is fair and reasonable business use, given your personal circumstances. It is often a good idea to seek approval of your estimates from the local VAT office before you send in your VAT return. If your circumstances do not change, you have then narrowed down the possibility of official disagreement at a later stage.

Charities suffer particularly from this restriction. They cannot recover VAT on their general overheads except to the extent they are incurred for their business, not their charitable, activities. Often this means restricting VAT by reference to business/non-business income. If a charity receives a great deal of voluntary funding, the resulting restriction may be severe. In such cases it may be possible to agree with Customs and Excise another method of calculating business input tax, perhaps based on costs or man hours devoted to business and non-business activities.

VAT invoices
In general, you should always be in possession of a valid VAT invoice from your supplier before claiming back VAT. If the supply is from a retailer and is not more than £50 in total, including VAT, this may be a less detailed tax invoice (see Chapter 5, Issuing Invoices). If it is over £50 in value you must hold a full tax invoice. This must show, amongst other things, the name and address of your business as the purchaser. It is essential to instruct employees, buying goods and services on the firm's behalf, to obtain tax invoices addressed to the business and not themselves. This applies equally to hotel invoices when employees stay overnight on the firm's business and to employees' removal expenses paid for by the firm.

There are only two items on which you may claim back VAT without holding some form of VAT invoice. These are payments for telephone calls made from public call boxes, and payments for off-street car parking.

Non-deductible business inputs
It has already been mentioned that the tax on certain business inputs cannot be reclaimed. The major non-deductible items are shown below.

Motor cars
VAT cannot be reclaimed on the purchase, including hire-purchase, of ordinary passenger cars and estate cars. This holds true irrespective of the amount of business use to which the car is put (for example, input tax cannot be reclaimed on a private car bought for use as a taxi).

This rule does not cover the following types of vehicles, VAT on which can be reclaimed from Customs and Excise if they are used for business purposes: motor cycles (with or without sidecars), single seat vehicles, vehicles capable of carrying twelve or more people, motor caravans, vans and commercial vehicles, London taxis.

However, a dealer in new motor cars may reclaim VAT on the cost of vehicles bought as part of his stock-in-trade.

If you sell a motor car used for the business you do not have to account for output tax unless you sell it for more than cost. In that case VAT is payable as $\frac{3}{23}$ times the difference between selling price and purchase price you paid.

Leased motor cars
Although VAT may not be reclaimed on a car purchased for the business, if a car is leased for business purposes VAT will be charged on the lease payments. This VAT can be reclaimed as input tax from Customs and Excise. However, this does not mean that leasing is any cheaper in VAT terms. The lessor will not have been able to reclaim the VAT charged to him when he purchased the vehicle. He will take this into account when setting the level of your lease payments.

Items installed by builders in new houses and buildings
If you are a builder who sells a newly constructed house, you must sell the house at the zero rate (ie without charging any VAT).

You will be able to reclaim VAT on most of the materials and fixtures used to construct the house. You may, however, have installed certain items which are not considered to be standard builders' fixtures. You are not allowed to reclaim input tax on these.

Since 1 June 1984 VAT has not been deductible on the following items: Fitted furniture (except kitchen units and work surfaces), cookers and domestic appliances, soft furnishings, gas fires not flued in, storage radiators, electric fires, extractor fans (except as the sole means of ventilating a wc).

Business entertaining

You may not deduct input VAT on entertaining business guests. You cannot deduct any input VAT on disallowed entertaining merely because your employees were present. However if while entertaining a guest away from your normal place of business you or your employee takes a meal you can deduct the VAT on the cost of your own or your employee's meal.

Food and accommodation provided to members of staff is not regarded as business entertaining.

Special cases concerning deduction of input tax

Motoring expenses

New rules apply to the amount of VAT which can be reclaimed on motoring expenses. Before this the rules on claiming back VAT on motoring expenses were quite complex. The main differences between the previous rules and the current rules were that sole proprietors and partners could not claim any VAT which related to their private motoring expenses. Businesses were able to claim back VAT on all motoring expenses incurred by the business for its employees, but had to account for VAT as output tax on the cost of petrol supplied to employees for their private motoring. How much restriction had to be made, and how much output tax paid was a matter for negotiation with the local VAT office.

The new rules

The new rules affect all VAT return periods beginning after 6 April 1987. From then on VAT can be reclaimed on all motoring expenses incurred for both business and private journeys. A private journey includes a journey from home to your normal place of business or work. A journey from home to any other place to conduct business is a business journey. VAT cannot be reclaimed on motoring expenses which are incurred for non-business journeys other than private journeys. For example, a charity cannot reclaim input tax on motoring expenses incurred in the course of its charitable activities. If a charity also runs a business and makes taxable supplies, it must come to some agreement with Customs and Excise over the end amount of input tax on motoring expenses which can be reclaimed.

VAT on road fuel used for private journeys

If you purchase petrol or road fuel for your own, or your employees' private journeys, either for their own cars or in a car provided by you for business reasons, you must account for output tax on the value of the road fuel used in this way on your VAT return.

If you make a charge which at least covers the full cost of the fuel used for private journeys, you should calculate your output tax as $\frac{3}{23}$ of the actual charge made. If you do not make such a charge, or the charge you make is less than the full cost of the fuel used, you must calculate the VAT due according to a scale which is reproduced below.

The scale charge

The VAT you pay depends on the amount of business mileage done by you, or your employees, in your VAT return period. A lesser charge applies if the business mileage done by a particular car user exceeds 4,500 miles in a three month period (1,500 miles in a one month period). If the lesser charge applies to a particular car user, you must keep a record of the business mileage done by that person's vehicle every VAT period in order to take advantage of it.

The VAT you will have to pay in respect of each car user to whom you supply petrol at less than cost may be found from the following table.

Standard scale

Cylinder capacity of vehicle	VAT payable Three month period £	One month period £
Up to 1400 cc	15.65	5.21
1401–2000 cc	19.56	6.52
Over 2000 cc	29.34	9.78

Reduced scale for business mileage of 1,500 miles or more per month

	VAT payable Three month period £	One month period £
Up to 1400 cc	7.82	2.60
1401–2000 cc	9.78	3.26
Over 2000 cc	14.73	4.95

If a car user changes car in the middle of a VAT period, so that person moves from one cylinder capacity band to another, you should apportion the VAT payable over the period between the two bands on a time basis. Otherwise VAT is payable for the whole period on the highest band.

For example, an employee changes at the end of month 1 in a three monthly VAT period from a 1500 cc car to a 1200 cc car.

The VAT payable is $\frac{1}{3} \times £19.56 + \frac{2}{3} \times 15.65 = £16.95$

Otherwise the VAT payable will be £19.56

Charges for the use of motor vehicles

If you charge an employee for the use of a company car you must account for output tax on the amount charged. If you charge an employee for the use of a vehicle and supply him with free petrol, you will have to account for VAT on the full value of the charge you make plus the appropriate scale charge for the use of fuel.

If instead you charge your employee for the full cost of petrol provided for his private use, plus a lesser charge for the use of the vehicle, you only have to account for VAT on the actual charge you make.

Records you need to keep

If you charge a business car user for the full cost of the fuel provided for private motoring you should keep a record of the charge made. You may have to justify to Customs and Excise that the charge made reasonably covered the amount of fuel provided.

If you have to use the scale charge you must keep a record of:

i   the number of vehicles for which free or below cost fuel is supplied;
ii   the cylinder capacity of each vehicle;
iii   the name of the person using each vehicle;
iv   a record of the business mileage done by any vehicle for which you are claiming the reduced charge.

Mileage allowances

If you pay a mileage allowance to your employees for the business mileage they do, you may claim as input tax $\frac{3}{23}$ of the amount intended to cover the cost of road fuel. This should be reasonably close to the estimates of per mileage fuel cost published by the major motoring organisations for cars of different cylinder capacities. If you are in doubt about the amount you estimate as fuel cost check your figures with the AA, RAC or the local VAT office. You can only claim back VAT on the fuel element of a mileage allowance and not on the total allowance if it is intended to cover repairs and maintenance, insurance etc.

No input tax claimed

You can by agreement with Customs and Excise, not claim any input tax back on petrol provided to employees. If you do this you will not be required to use the scale charge. However there can be very few businesses where this alternative would offer any real advantage.

Supplies bought by your employees

If your employees buy goods or services on your behalf and in the course of your business, then you may reclaim input tax on these purchases, provided you can show in your records that your employees have been reimbursed. This covers such things as an employee paying for food and lodging whilst away on a business trip.

If, however, you pay your employees a fixed expense allowance, you cannot reclaim input tax on the goods and services bought by your employees with such an allowance.

Staff entertainment

The provision of food or accommodation for staff is for business purposes. Any VAT you incur on the cost of entertaining staff may be treated as input tax. Furthermore no output tax need be accounted for on the supply of entertainment to staff unless you actually charge them for it.

Business gifts and gifts to staff

You may deduct VAT in full on the value of any gifts given away for business purposes or to members of staff. However, if the cost of any gift exceeds £10 in value, or if it forms part of a series of gifts to one individual, then you must account for output tax on the cost of each gift. The cost to you is the price you paid for the gift excluding VAT.

Domestic accommodation

When a building is used solely for business purposes, eg a warehouse, barn or lock up shop, any VAT incurred on the furnishing, upkeep or repair of the building may be treated as input tax. When the building used for business purposes is also the domestic residence of the owner of the business, or his employee, eg a farmhouse, tied cottage or shop with living accommodation above, there are rules to be observed with regard to the claiming of input tax. These are outlined below.

Sole proprietors

For the sole proprietor it is sometimes obvious what can be reclaimed and what cannot, eg VAT on an office desk and equipment can, but VAT on your favourite personal armchair cannot. Difficulties arise with costs incurred partly for private, partly for business purposes, such as repairs to the building fabric, or to central heating systems etc. In these cases you must make a fair apportionment of any VAT charged between business and non-business use.

The amount you can reclaim will vary according to circumstances. If you are a farmer, architect, or accountant, working from home, you will not, as a general rule, be allowed to reclaim more than one-third of any VAT charged on the upkeep of the property. If your residence is also a guest house the proportion allowed to you will be greater.

In all cases, review your circumstances, arrive at an estimate of the business use to which your home is put, and then try to agree your conclusions with the local VAT office.

Employees

If you have an employee, including a director of a limited company, living in a house that you own or rent, you may treat as business input tax any VAT that you incur on the upkeep, maintenance or furnishing of that house provided the employee occupies the house for the purpose of your business. If you allow any goods in the house to pass to the ownership of your employee, you must account for output tax on the cost of those goods to the business. Be careful, however, when the person living in the house is the person in control of the business, eg, the director and major shareholder of a small company. Customs and Excise may well argue that in such circumstances VAT on domestic costs is not incurred for the purpose of any business carried on by the company

Partnerships

Where a partnership owns a house which is occupied by one partner, VAT incurred on the upkeep of the house will not be allowed as input tax unless the house is being used to carry on some of the partnership's business activities. In this case input tax must be apportioned in the same way as described for sole proprietors.

Constructing buildings

Where you are constructing a building yourself which is to be used only for business purposes, you will be allowed to reclaim VAT on the cost of building materials and services engaged in its planning or construction. If you are not already registered for VAT, but are planning to construct a building in order to start a business, you may be able to register as an intending trader (see page 9). If the building you are planning is a house, then unless you construct houses for sale as part of your normal business activities you must not reclaim VAT in the normal way, ie on your VAT returns. You may be allowed to submit a claim under the 'Do-it-yourself' Homebuilders Scheme (see page 15).

Conclusion

We have discussed the meaning of input tax and the difference between business and non-business inputs. By following the guidelines in this chapter you can arrive at a total of business input tax which you have a right to reclaim. If all your sales or outputs are taxable (that is zero rated or positive rated), you can reclaim this total business input tax in full. If any of your sales are exempt you may have to make an apportionment (see section on partial exemption, Chapter 13).

You are, of course, required by law to keep evidence in support of any tax claim you make upon Customs and Excise. This means retaining tax invoices and keeping proper records.

Refunds of VAT from Europe
If you are registered for VAT in the UK and incur expenses or purchase goods on which you are charged VAT by suppliers established in other member states of the European Community, for example the expenses you incur on a business trip in order to inspect or make a purchase of machinery, or to obtain orders for exports, you cannot claim back the VAT you have been charged by foreign suppliers on your UK VAT returns. You may, however, be able to make a claim for VAT from the tax authority of the member state in which you were charged VAT.

The claim is subject to certain conditions:

You must be registered for VAT in the UK;

You must not be established for business purposes, nor make supplies of goods or services, in the member state from whom you are claiming back VAT.

The form on which you can make a claim can be obtained from any local VAT office.

The VAT office will supply you with an English language version but you must complete it in block capitals *in the language of the member state from whom you are claiming back VAT*. This may mean that it is not worth incurring the expense of translating the form into a foreign language unless the claim is large enough to justify doing so. In addition, very small claims under given monetary limits in each member state (equivalent to about £16) will not be entertained. A claim for refund of VAT must be made for a calendar year and must be made within six months of the end of the year in which the VAT was charged. Claims for periods of not less than three months may be made if sufficiently large (where the VAT claimed is more than a stated monetary limit equivalent to £130).

Some member states will now allow refunds of certain kinds of expenses. These are, commonly, hotel accommodation, food and drink, entertaining and petrol. Fuller details of the refund scheme can be obtained from your local VAT office and in Customs and Excise VAT Notice 723. Refunds of VAT cannot yet be obtained from either Greece or Portugal. Spain is apparently giving refunds of VAT but details of how the scheme operates are not generally available in the UK. If in doubt, you could make enquiries of either the Spanish Embassy or the relevant tax authorities in Spain.

It may now be possible for UK businesses to obtain refunds of VAT and similar indirect taxes from countries which enter into reciprocal arrangements with the UK. Check with the trade attaché of the Embassy of the country you are going to visit before you go.

CHAPTER TWELVE

VAT and the importer

General
Many foreign goods have established markets in the UK today. A large number of firms of varying sizes make it their business to buy goods from foreign suppliers and resell them to the home market. Other firms may have only sporadic or one-off dealings with foreign suppliers. Whatever the frequency at which a firm buys goods from abroad, as soon as it takes responsibility for goods being shipped into this country it has become involved in the business of importation.

Importation is quite simply the act of bringing into the UK goods from other countries. The goods concerned are referred to as 'imports' and the person responsible for bringing them in as the 'importer'.

If you are an importer of goods into the UK you must follow the special procedures laid down by Customs and Excise. It is not within the scope of this book to explain general customs procedure; suffice it to say that the process involved is termed 'making an entry'. Advice on this can be obtained from your local Customs and Excise office or from a reputable shipping agent.

Imports and VAT
Customs and Excise duties are levied on certain types of goods, dependent on their country of origin. VAT is also levied according to the rules used in the United Kingdom concerning standard and zero rating of VAT on commodities, irrespective of the country of origin. For example VAT at 15% is charged on cars whether they are exported from Germany or Japan, whereas tomatoes are zero rated whether they come from the Canaries or the Channel Islands.

Where VAT is chargeable it is levied on the full value of the imported goods including any charges for commission, freight, packing, insurance and duties of Customs and Excise. The value of the goods is for VAT purposes the price paid in an arm's length transaction. Where the buyer and seller are connected persons and the buyer cannot reclaim VAT in full, VAT is payable on the open market value of the imported goods.

Imports and the VAT registered person

Accounting for VAT
If you are a VAT registered person and have had to import goods for the purpose of carrying on your business you will have made a declaration of importation of goods to Customs and Excise. The form used for this declaration will include a copy for VAT purposes. This copy will form part of your VAT records and must be retained as evidence for reclaiming VAT.

VAT is payable at the time of importation or removal from bonded warehouse. If you are a regular importer or bonded warehouse user you may be allowed to postpone payment of VAT under the duty deferment system. Customs and Excise will require a deposit or guarantee of at least twice the amount of VAT you would expect to pay in any month.

Under this system payment of the VAT on imports in any month is made by direct debit from your bank account on the 15th day of the month following.

You must still retain the VAT copy of the Customs entry or computer generated 'period' entry as evidence of input tax. If you are using the VAT and duty deferment system you will be sent deferment statements. These show the amount of VAT deferred on imports in one month, which is payable in the next. These do not count as evidence of input tax. You should ensure that you have appropriate VAT copies of entries corresponding to the details shown on the deferment statement. If you have not received copy entries for any of the amounts shown as payable on the deferment statement you should immediately take the matter up with your shipping agent or the Customs and Excise office responsible for processing the entry form. You can claim VAT on imports as input tax in the period in which the importation is made.

Postal imports—value not exceeding £1,300

You are not required to pay VAT immediately on postal imports (other than Datapost packets) which do not exceed £1,300 in value provided they are accompanied by a customs declaration showing your VAT registration number. You account for any tax due in box 1 of your VAT return.

Relief from VAT on importation

Certain types of goods are relieved from VAT and duty on importation. These include:

a   Agricultural products and animals.
b   Capital goods and equipment used for a business carried on abroad which has ceased.
c   Goods imported by charities.
d   Donated medical equipment.
e   Goods imported for exhibition purposes.
f   Goods for testing.
g   Goods for the blind and handicapped.
h   Goods purchased from private individuals in other EC states.
i   Products for health research.
j   Machines to improve industrial, scientific or medical techniques.
k   Copyright applications.
l   Recorded material sent free of charge to transfer information.
m   Any consignment of goods less than £6 in value sent in the Post (excluding tobacco, alcohol and perfume).
n   Personal property permanently imported.
o   Trade promotion goods.
p   Reimported goods including goods sent abroad for process or treatment.
q   Small non-commercial consignments.
r   Works of art and collectors' pieces.
s   Goods returned to the supplier because they are not according to contract.

More details of these and other reliefs can be obtained from your local Customs and Excise office.

Temporary imports

From 1 January 1986 any registered person who temporarily imports goods for his business may reclaim the VAT payable on importation on his VAT returns. This saves having to claim specific relief from Customs and Excise which requires the importer to provide security. A specific claim must be lodged with Customs and Excise to claim relief from duty, and for unregistered persons to claim relief from VAT. Customs and Excise will require security from the importer in the form of a deposit or bank guarantee, and evidence that the goods have been subsequently re-exported.

Some goods may be temporarily imported without payment of VAT or security. These include goods imported for repair, means of transport, containers and pallets, and personal effects. Such goods must normally be re-exported within certain time limits. More details can be obtained from your local Customs and Excise office.

Goods in transit in the UK between one port or airport and another may be imported free of duty and VAT. Customs and Excise will require security for both.

Relief from VAT paid in other EC countries

When you import goods into the UK which have been acquired, VAT paid, in another member state of the EC you can claim relief against the VAT you have to pay on importing the goods into this country. The amount of relief is either the VAT charged when the goods were acquired or the appropriate VAT fraction of the price you acquired the goods for if that is less—for example you may have acquired the goods second hand. If this figure is greater than the VAT payable on importation then you do not pay any VAT at all but you cannot claim a refund. To claim the relief you must produce an invoice or other evidence showing that VAT has been paid in the other member state and you must be able to satisfy Customs and Excise that the VAT has not been repaid in that member state. See VAT leaflet 702/1 for further details.

Reverse charge services

Where a taxable person receives certain services from abroad he must account for tax on those services as if he had supplied them himself in the UK. In other words they are subject to a reverse VAT charge.

The services affected by this reverse charge are listed in Schedule 3 to the VAT Act 1983 and include:

a   Transfers of copyrights, patents, licences and trade marks.
b   Advertising services.
c   Services of consultants, engineers, lawyers, accountants, data processing, provision of information (but not if these services relate to transactions involving land).
d   Agreement to refrain from any business activity or the exercise of any right mentioned in **a**.
e   Banking, financial and insurance services.
f   Supply of staff.
g   Hire of goods other than means of transport.
h   Services rendered in procuring any service comprised in **a–g**.

If you receive any of the above services from someone who belongs overseas and the service would be taxable if it was supplied by a person belonging in the UK, you must account for output tax on the value of the supply, ie at 15% of the price paid for the service.

At the same time you may treat the VAT amount as input tax. The two VAT amounts will cancel out on your VAT return, unless you are a partly exempt person (see Chapter 13), in which case you may not be able to recover this input tax in full.

The reverse charge is not applicable to services which are either exempt or zero rated under UK VAT law, eg the payment of interest is not subject to the reverse VAT charge.

Reverse charge services and unregistered persons from 1 April 1987

Until 1 April 1987, persons not registered for VAT because they were making exempt supplies could ignore reverse charge services. Until then reverse charge services only affected those already registered for VAT.

Now, from 1 April 1987, a person who carries on in business in the UK supplying goods or services which are wholly or mainly exempt from VAT, will be required to register if he pays overseas suppliers for services subject to the reverse charge which, together with any taxable supplies he might make in the UK, exceed the VAT registration limit. This means that from 1 April 1987 previously exempt persons caught by this provision will have to apply the reverse charge procedures explained above to their payments to overseas suppliers of reverse charge services. In all probability they will be unable to reclaim the VAT 'reverse charged' as deductible input tax.

CHAPTER THIRTEEN

The partly exempt business

Exempt outputs and partial exemption

It has already been mentioned that some supplies are exempt from VAT by law. This affects in the main people who supply certain kinds of services. Examples are services concerning:

a Land—eg income from rented property; sales of land and buildings.
b Insurance—eg the services of an authorised insurer, insurance agent or broker.
c Betting and gaming—eg collection of bets by a turf-accountant; sale of lottery tickets.
d Finance—eg credit charges made to customers over and above the value of goods supplied.
e Health—eg services provided by registered doctors and nursing staff.
f Burial and cremation—eg services provided by undertakers.

Exemption from VAT might at first sound like a good idea, but its implications are usually less than welcome. Anyone who makes only exempt supplies (see Chapter 3: Exempt Supplies) cannot register for VAT and thus cannot recover input tax on any supplies he purchases for his business. Anyone who is exempt from VAT either has to bear the VAT on his expenses as a cost to his business, or pass them on as best he can as a 'hidden tax' in the price of his goods or services.

A person who makes both taxable and exempt supplies in the course of his business is termed a 'partly exempt' person. Only a person who is fully taxable, ie makes only taxable supplies, can recover input tax in full. Anyone who is partly exempt has a problem in determining how much of his input tax he is able to claim back in any VAT period.

Partial exemption—The new rules from 1 April 1987

From 1 April 1987 the law changed to affect the way in which partly exempt persons recover VAT on their inputs. Broadly, instead of looking at the level of exempt outputs to determine whether or not input tax has to be restricted, a partly exempt person is required to identify how much input tax relates to taxable supplies. This is called 'direct attribution'. The input tax which is attributable to taxable supplies may be reclaimed, whilst the input tax which is attributable to exempt supplies, beyond certain tolerance limits, cannot be reclaimed.

Input tax attributable to an exempt supply is called 'exempt input tax' and is not recoverable whether it relates to an exempt supply in a current or future VAT period. Direct attribution in practice means that all partly exempt businesses will be required to perform direct costing exercises in their accounts, allocating costs and expenses not just to different cost centres and departments, but to specific supplies within such departments.

If input tax cannot be 'attributed' in this fashion then it must be apportioned to determine the amount which is attributable to taxable supplies (and therefore recoverable). This will affect input tax on general overheads and other expenses which cannot be neatly and tidily allocated to a particular supply.

The law requires that an apportionment should be based on the amount of use to which such inputs are put. In other words, if 50% of input tax on general overhead is incurred for making taxable supplies, then 50% of such input tax is recoverable. The law does not go on to say how to determine the amount of use to which an input is put. This is left to the judgement of the taxpayer. The prudent taxpayer will of course discuss any proposal for apportioning input tax with Customs and Excise before carrying it out. Customs and Excise suggest that whatever the percentage of your total input tax is in fact directly attributable to taxable supplies, you may also treat as attributable to taxable supplies the same percentage of your unattributable input tax.

Example:

	£	%
In a VAT period you incur total input tax	10,000	100
Directly attributable to taxable supplies	3,000	30
Directly attributable to exempt supplies	2,500	25
Unattributable input tax	4,500	45

Using Customs and Excise's suggested method you would treat as attributable to taxable supplies 30% of the £4,500 of input tax not directly attributable. You would therefore reclaim £1,350 as input tax attributable to taxable supplies in addition to the £3,000 which you can directly attribute. This method is somewhat weighted against the taxpayer and anyone faced with the problem of partial exemption should consider alternative methods of apportioning input tax on overheads before resorting to the method suggested by Customs and Excise.

Where input tax cannot easily be apportioned according to use, Customs and Excise will allow the residual input tax to be apportioned according to the value of taxable supplies using a method similar to the standard method which existed prior to 1 April 1987. Agreement should be obtained from Customs and Excise in writing before using this method.

Current special methods

Any business which had agreed a special method with Customs and Excise before 1 April 1987 will in general be allowed to continue to use it. In addition Customs and Excise continue to have the power to approve special methods in the future.

Exempt input tax which can be reclaimed

If the exempt input tax relates to:

i money on deposit;
ii rental income, providing the input tax attributable to it is less than £1,000 in a tax year and the landlord does not make any exempt supplies other than i above and iii–v below;
iii commission for arranging insurance;
iv commissions for arranging mortgages, hire purchase or credit transactions;
v the assignment of a debt by the person providing the original goods or services;
   it may be reclaimed.

This provision does not apply to business in the financial sector.

If exempt input tax in any period amounts to less than any one of the following:
i   £100 per month on average;
ii £250 per month on average and less than 50% of all input tax;
iii £500 per month on average and less than 25% of all input tax;
    the exempt input tax can be recovered.

Exempt input tax relating to any of the supplies listed above is not to be included in calculating the above limits.

The *de minimis* inputs rules seem sufficiently generous to allow most small businesses making exempt supplies to escape the regulations. However, most businesses making both taxable and exempt supplies will be required to carry out the accounting exercises necessary to determine whether or not any input tax incurred in making exempt supplies is sufficiently low to be recovered. The burden is on the taxpayer to prove his exempt input tax is sufficiently low.

Many medium sized to large businesses which previously would have escaped the rigours of partial exemption because of the relatively more generous outputs rules are now partly exempt and must comply with the partial exemption rules.

Adjustment of input tax

The amount of deductible input tax must be determined for each tax period, ie, the period of the VAT return. In addition an adjustment must be made at the end of each tax year, ending on 31 March, 30 April or 31 May, depending on the period of the taxpayer's VAT returns. The adjustment is effectively carried out by taking the input tax figures for the whole year and recalculating the amount of input tax deductible, treating each previous VAT period in the year as a provisional calculation. In most cases only the apportioned input tax will be adjusted, and only when there is a change in the proportion of use. It should even be possible to agree with Customs and Excise a proportion for the whole year in advance. The agreed proportion would only need to be adjusted if there was a change in circumstances affecting, for example, the mix of supplies or inputs.

Provisional allocations of input tax

Where inputs may be acquired for the purpose of making taxable supplies at some future date, the input tax may be provisionally allocated to taxable supplies in the period in which the inputs are acquired. Under the annual adjustment rules such input tax would remain deductible even if the intended taxable supplies had not been made in the taxpayer's VAT year. If in the following year the intended taxable supplies do not materialise or the inputs are diverted to exempt supplies, the input tax recovered would not be affected by the following year's annual adjustment.

There is therefore a provision which requires an adjustment of input tax which has been provisionally allocated to taxable supplies and deducted in one VAT year and used in a following VAT year to make exempt supplies. The adjustment must be carried out if the change in use occurs within six years from the beginning of the VAT period in which the input tax was deducted. The adjustment is made in accordance with the method used by the taxpayer to attribute input tax in the period in which the input tax was deducted. So if there is a change in method in the following year when the inputs are put to a different use, the input tax adjustment is not affected by the change in method.

The adjustment is entered on the VAT return for the period following that in which the change of use took place. The adjustment should also be carried out, and the same rules apply, when input tax is provisionally attributed to an exempt supply and the inputs are used in a future VAT year for making taxable supplies.

Capital goods scheme

The capital goods scheme will come into effect on 1 April 1990. It will apply to capital items brought into use on or after 1 April 1990 and used for a non-taxable purpose. The scheme will only affect relatively large partly exempt businesses and it will only apply to computers and items of computer equipment worth £50,000 or more and land and buildings worth £250,000 or more.

The taxpayer will be required to adjust input tax on capital items over a five year period—ten years in the case of land and buildings—if there is a change in the proportion to which the asset is used in making taxable supplies. The adjustment is made to one fifth* or the input tax of the capital item over a five year period* beginning with when the item is first acquired or put to use.

For example:
Input tax on computer	£10,000
Percentage of taxable use in first period	30%
Input tax originally recovered	£3,000
Percentage of taxable use in following tax year	50%

Adjustment required:

$$\frac{£10,000}{5} \times (50 - 30)\% = £2,000 \times 20\% = £400$$

In this example Customs and Excise owe the taxpayer £400.

Self supplies

An exempt or partly exempt person is sometimes liable to account for VAT on self supplied goods and services. If he is liable to account for output tax on the self supply he can treat the same amount as input tax but he can only claim so much of it as is attributable to making taxable supplies. Any VAT on the cost of goods and services used to produce the self supplies may be recovered in full.

If an exempt or partly exempt person produces stationery in house for use in his business and the cost of producing it exceeds the VAT registration limits he must account for output tax on the value of any that is liable to the standard rate. As a rule of thumb forms and records that are produced for completion are standard rated but advertising and publicity material is not.

From 1 August 1989 a person who lets out a new building without opting to tax the rent or uses it at any time for exempt or non taxable business within ten years of its completion is liable to account for VAT on the cost of the building. Similar rules will apply to extensions of, annexes to, reconstructions and enlargements of existing buildings. The new rules will not apply where the value of the building or work would be less than £100,000. (See also Chapter 3 under 'Land'.)

---

* one tenth and ten years in the case of land and buildings.

CHAPTER FOURTEEN

Records and accounts

General
The actual accounts you will need or are advised to keep will vary considerably according to the sort of business you run.

There are a variety of systems available commercially for all types of business. Alternatively, you may devise your own system. Ready made systems that are available range from computerised systems to simple cash books that are readily available from most stationers. Most cash books will contain instructions on how to use the book. Certainly it is something you ought to get well organised before you commence trading. You can discuss the sort of accounts you will need for the business as a whole (and not just for VAT purposes) with a reputable accountant who should be able to produce your yearly profit and loss accounts and balance sheet and your tax computations.

The system you choose for your business as a whole should be suitable or adaptable to your VAT situation. If not, separate accounts for VAT may be kept, although this may create further paperwork for you.

We have already outlined some accounting requirements and examples of suitable systems in certain cases, eg for retail and second-hand schemes (see Chapters 9 and 10). Invoice and gross takings requirements have also been discussed (see Chapter 5).

We must now look at your position regarding the legal requirements of accounting for VAT.

The law
Much of the law regarding books and records for VAT purposes is very general. You must keep such books and records as the Commissioners of Customs and Excise may require. So, if they feel the accounts you currently maintain for VAT purposes do not produce the information required by law in a readily available form, they may require you to keep the records in another form. They might make this sort of direction following a visit to inspect your accounts.

The records you are required to keep include your sales and purchase invoices, any credit notes given or received, delivery notes and order notes, your books of account, records of daily takings including till rolls, your annual profit and loss account and balance sheet, documentation relating to exports and imports, business bank statements, and a VAT account.

You are now required to keep your VAT records for six years, although a lesser period may be allowed on application to the VAT office. You will need to show that it is impractical to keep them for this length of time and that you can convert the original documents into another suitable form to satisfy the Customs and Excise. This might be the case with a very large business generating vast quantities of paperwork. The business might wish to store the information on computers, microfilm, or similar facilities. If this is the case the storage systems must be capable of making information readily available.

Whatever your accounting system, large or small, you must be able to show how you arrive at your declared figures for input and output tax. You must, furthermore, be able to produce supporting documentation for your book entries.

Customs and Excise may also request the maintenance of any VAT related documents and records, eg profit and loss accounts and balance sheets. Books and records must be made available for Customs and Excise to inspect at a reasonable time and for a reasonable period.

Customs and Excise may impose penalties for failing to keep adequate records or to preserve them for the required time. The penalties are described in Chapter 16. 'Your legal rights and obligations'.

Records which you need to keep

You are required to keep a record for each VAT period of the value of all your taxable supplies including any zero rated supplies you have made. You are also required to keep a record of the value of any exempt supplies you have made in the VAT period. You need to keep a separate record of any exports you have made, and of any self supplied goods, reverse charge services from overseas suppliers, free gifts, bonus goods given to customers and the cost of goods put to private use and on which VAT is due. You should also keep a record of any credits for VAT which you have allowed to customers. You must keep a record of all the taxable supplies you have received from your customers in the VAT period and of any credits for VAT you have received, and the value of any imports you have made.

For each VAT period you must keep a VAT account. This should be in two parts. One part should show the output tax due from you on your taxable supplies (less any VAT credits you have given) plus any VAT due on reverse charge services from overseas suppliers and on self supplies and on any postal imports you made during the VAT period. The second part should show the VAT you are entitled to claim back. This is the input tax on the supplies you received in your business (less any VAT credits due to you) plus VAT paid on any imports you made for your business, plus any tax you are able to claim back on reverse charge services from overseas and on any self supplies. It is also sensible to keep a copy of the VAT return which you send in to Customs and Excise.

If you are a retailer you must keep a record of the retail scheme calculation you carried out to work out the tax due on your retail sales. You must also keep a record of any calculation, such as a partial exemption calculation, which you had to do to arrive at the total input tax you are able to claim on your VAT return.

An example of a VAT account is shown overleaf.

Accounting for VAT without detailed accounts

Customs and Excise require that at the end of each VAT period you account for VAT on all the goods or services that you have supplied and received in that period. The date of supply and receipt is governed by the tax point rules explained in Chapter 6. For most businesses in general the tax point is the date an invoice is issued.

If your normal daily records are not geared to do this you need not keep an elaborate book-keeping system specifically for VAT. As long as all your supplies are recorded on tax invoices, and the invoices show all the information that Customs and Excise require, your records need not be any more than add lists of your invoices.

You will need:
a To file all your invoices for one VAT period together.
b To make add lists in the sequence of the filed invoices.

Your add list for outputs must show in the total:
a The total amount of VAT charged for the period.

A VAT ACCOUNT

PERIOD FROM 1 JULY 1989 to 30 SEPTEMBER 1989

VAT DEDUCTIBLE – INPUT TAX		VAT PAYABLE – OUTPUT TAX	
VAT you have been charged on your purchases	£	VAT you have charged on your sales	
October	615.23	October	780.23
November	324.51	November	685.45
December	519.75	December	687.42
	1,459.49		2,153.10
VAT on imports	96.85	VAT due on postal imports	6.85
Overdeclarations of VAT from previous periods, but not those notified by Customs and Excise (This includes relief on bad debts)	350.75	Underdeclarations of VAT from previous periods but not those notified by Customs and Excise	173.20
	1,907.09		2,333.15
Less:		Less:	
VAT on credits you have received from suppliers	27.50	VAT on credits you have allowed your customers	23.00
TOTAL TAX DEDUCTIBLE	1,879.59	TOTAL TAX PAYABLE	2,310.15
		Less: TOTAL TAX DEDUCTIBLE	1,879.59
		TAX PAYABLE TO CUSTOMS AND EXCISE	430.56

Reproduced from Customs and Excise leaflet 700/21/87

b The total value of all taxable supplies (including zero rate outputs).
c The total value of any exempt outputs.

Your add list for inputs must show:

a The total amount of VAT you are reclaiming for the period.
b The total amount of all your inputs for the period.

Cash accounting for small businesses

From 1 October 1987, businesses with a turnover of less than £250,000 pa may account for VAT on a cash basis. The £250,000 taxable turnover limit is before VAT and excludes the value of any capital assets which you have sold and which were previously used in your business. Businesses wishing to use this option will have to apply to the local VAT office. Once a person has obtained approval to use the scheme he will be required to use cash accounting for at least two years. You will only be allowed to use the scheme if you are up to date with all your VAT returns and payments and have paid any penalties due from you, if you have not committed a VAT offence of a serious nature nor have been expelled from the cash accounting scheme in the last three years. There is no point in applying to use the scheme if you receive regular repayments of VAT. You may apply to use the scheme if you have not been registered for VAT before.

If your taxable turnover increases above £250,000 per year you can continue to use the scheme as long as your taxable turnover has not exceeded £312,500. If it has you will need to convince Customs and Excise that your taxable turnover is not going to be more than £250,000 for the next twelve months if you wish to continue using the scheme.

You must be able to cross reference your sales and purchase VAT invoices to evidence of receipts and payments—your bank records and cash accounts for example. You must have receipted VAT invoices for payments made in cash and you must receipt your sales invoices if you accept cash as payment. If you sell or buy goods under hire purchase, credit sale and conditional sale agreements, these must be recorded outside the scheme. You must account for VAT on such transactions according to the normal tax point rules.

Cash accounting means effectively accounting for VAT on a cash paid and received basis, as opposed to the general requirement to account for VAT according to the date of the supply or tax point (which in practice in the majority of cases is the date an invoice is issued). It is of benefit to smaller non-retail concerns, particularly those whose inputs subject to VAT are relatively low, mostly in the service sector. VAT on supplies does not have to be paid to Customs and Excise until after payment has been received from the customer. This effectively gives relief from VAT on bad debts outside the formal bad debt relief scheme. It also means that VAT cannot be claimed on inputs until you have paid your supplier.

This may be disadvantageous if you anticipate large capital outlay over the next year or two and are spreading the means of payment to your supplier over a lengthy period. It should not, however, adversely affect such plans where payment to the supplier is made by borrowing from a third party, say a bank.

The cash accounting scheme does not benefit retailers, most of whom account for VAT already on a cash received basis. They have the advantage of accounting for VAT on inputs on the basis of invoices received.

The cash accounting scheme is well worth considering if you are running a small service business but do be wary of some of the complications which it presents in terms of extra book keeping.

CHAPTER FIFTEEN

Completing returns

General
VAT returns must be accurately completed and submitted by the date stated on them. Failure to comply with this may lead to assessment of the VAT due by Customs and Excise. It can also lead to the imposition of penalties or a default surcharge. Sending in VAT returns and payments by the due date is now of vital importance. This is discussed further in Chapter 16.

Periods covered
VAT returns usually cover a three month period. Returns covering one month are normally given if you expect to receive frequent repayments of VAT because, for example, you make only zero rated supplies.

You can also request your VAT return dates to coincide with any particular accounting arrangements you may have. For example where you wish to match the dates of VAT returns to coincide with the dates of your financial year.

Completion
An example of a VAT return is given on page 94 with notes on how to complete it.

In its most basic form the VAT return can be divided up into five sections, each of which becomes a declaration by you of:
a   The tax due on your sales (output tax).
b   Tax that you may reclaim on your business expenditure (input tax).
c   The difference between a and b. This represents the amount due to or from Customs and Excise. If your output tax exceeds your input tax you will *owe* the balance. If your input tax exceeds your output tax you are *owed* the balance.
d   Your sales net of VAT.
e   Your purchases net of VAT.

As you can see in the example on page 94, there are boxes to adjust for errors in previous periods.

There are also boxes to tick if you have used a retail scheme to calculate output tax or, claimed bad debt relief, or you make exempt supplies.

You must not qualify a VAT return, eg by writing anything on the form that affects the declaration you have to sign.

Declarations and payments

What you *declare* on a VAT return as due by or to you for the period may be something different from what you actually pay or are repaid.

You may have received an assessment of tax due because you have not sent in a VAT return. You may have paid this and subsequently sent in the return. You must not enter the payment of the assessment on the VAT return to adjust the amount payable or repayable. The adjustment boxes on the return are for errors made in declaration of tax due in previous periods, not over and under payments. The function of the VAT return is to make a declaration of the tax due or repayable. Payments and receipts form a separate function. The two must not be confused. If the amount of tax you declare on the VAT return as due to Customs and Excise is greater than an assessment you may have paid for the same period you should send the balance to Customs and Excise. If the tax due on your VAT return is less than an assessment you have paid for the same period Customs and Excise will repay the balance to you, provided you have no other outstanding VAT returns or payments.

Currently, errors in VAT declared on previous returns are self-adjusted by the taxpayer in either box 2 or box 5 of the VAT return. This is to change from a date to be announced either late in 1989 or early in 1990. From that date, errors made on previous VAT returns must be declared to Customs and Excise on a separate form. If the taxpayer has over-declared VAT in a previous period, Customs and Excise may reject a claim for it to be refunded, if they can show that the taxpayer would be unjustly enriched as a result. If a claim for a refund is rejected, the taxpayer can appeal to a VAT tribunal.

Payments and repayments

You can make payments by:

a   Cheque.
b   Credit transfer via bank or Giro. Customs and Excise will provide the appropriate forms on request.
c   Postal order.

Repayments to you will usually be made direct to your bank account if Customs and Excise have details of the Bank, Branch and account number (normally given when you register for VAT). Otherwise you will be sent a payable order.

Repayment supplement

Where a repayment return is submitted to Customs and Excise within 2 months of the end of the period, and Customs and Excise fail to direct repayment within 30 days of the end of the period or the date the return is received, if later, they will pay a supplement to compensate for the delay. The return must not show an error against the Customs and Excise of more than £100 in the repayment sum. The supplement is the greater of 5% of the repayment or £30.

The supplement is not always available, eg where a claim is for bad debt relief or DIY housebuilding scheme.

Annual accounting

From 1 July 1988 small businesses can make a single VAT return at the end of each year instead of the more normal four quarterly ones. Payment of VAT due is made by direct debit in nine equal instalments throughout the year with any balance being accounted for on the yearly return. You can use the scheme if your taxable turnover does not exceed £250,000 per year excluding VAT and excluding the value of any capital assets previously used in your business.

You must be registered for VAT for at least one year before you can use the scheme and you must be up to date with your VAT returns and payments of tax or penalties. You cannot use the scheme if you receive regular repayments of VAT. You must apply to your local VAT office to use the scheme on the form printed on the back of VAT Notice 732 Annual Accounting. You use the scheme for at least two years, subject to certain exceptions. You must inform Customs and Excise of any significant change in your business after starting to use the scheme.

You have to leave the scheme if your taxable turnover exceeds £312,500 unless you can convince Customs and Excise that your turnover is not going to be more than £250,000 in the next twelve months. You can leave the scheme at any time if you have been in it for at least two years. Customs and Excise will withdraw the use of the scheme from anyone who fails to meet any payments due or to make the annual return of tax by the required date or who breaches any of the conditions of the scheme.

The nine direct debits are set at one tenth of your total VAT payments in the last year. These are adjusted to take into account any anticipated changes in turnover or trading. You should tell Customs and Excise if you expect your turnover to increase or decrease. The first payment by direct debit is due at the end of the fourth month of the first year in which you use the scheme. The final payment by direct debit is made at the end of that year.

You only submit one VAT return under the scheme. The annual VAT return looks no different from any other VAT return. The return must reach Customs and Excise by the end of the second month after the end of the scheme year. To complete the annual VAT return you must use your records of supplies made and received as well as output tax and input tax for the whole year. You must send the balancing payment with (or claim any balancing repayment on) the annual return. This will be the difference between the net tax due on the return and the total of your nine payments of VAT by direct debit. You must still send in the annual return each year even if no balancing payment or repayment is due. After the end of your scheme year Customs and Excise will send you a statement showing the estimate of VAT due from you for the next year, the direct debit amounts and the due date for the annual return and balancing payment.

You can use the annual accounting scheme together with a retail scheme. If you do so you only need to do one retail scheme calculation at the end of each year. Retail schemes B1, D and J require annual adjustments so for these schemes the date you would normally carry out your retail scheme adjustment must be the same as the end of your annual accounting year. If you are partly exempt the end of your annual accounting year must coincide with the date you are required to carry out your partial exemption annual adjustment. You will only need to carry out one partial exemption calculation using your figures for the whole year. This scheme may be used in conjunction with the cash accounting scheme.

The scheme may help those who find VAT creates a cash flow problem when it requires payment. A single VAT return per year reduces the burden caused by filling in a VAT return every quarter. On the other hand completing a VAT return for a whole year's trading figures could be a mammoth task unless accounts have been meticulously kept.

Late returns and payments of VAT

Failure to send in VAT returns or to pay VAT when due may now result in financial penalties being imposed by Customs. Businesses now need to be more disciplined in the way accounting information is kept and returned for VAT purposes. More details of the penalties can be found in the next chapter 'Your legal rights and obligations'.

Example: How to complete a VAT return

Mr Smith is a retailer who can separate his takings into the two VAT rates. His records for the quarter ending 28 February 1987 show the following:

	Takings Including VAT 15%		Including VAT 0%		Exports
April	1,150		500		—
May	2,300		500		—
June	3,450		500		200
Total	(A) 6,900	(B)	1,500	(C)	200

	Purchases Excluding VAT		VAT		Imports Excluding VAT		VAT
April	2,000		200		—		—
May	1,500		200		100		15
June	1,500		100		—		—
	(D) 5,000	(E)	500	(F)	100	(G)	15

Mr Smith then calculates his output tax for the quarter (VAT due on sales)

$$\text{Output tax} = (A) \times \tfrac{3}{23} \quad (H) \; 900$$

CROWN COPYRIGHT

KEY TO FILLING IN FORM VAT 100 (overleaf)

BOX 1 VAT due on sales ENTER (H)
BOX 2 VAT underdeclared in previous periods and discovered by yourself (owed to Customs and Excise).
BOX 3 TOTAL BOXES 1–2
BOX 4 VAT reclaimable on purchases and imports ENTER (E) + (G)
BOX 5 VAT overdeclared in previous periods discovered by yourself (owed by Customs and Excise) and VAT claimed on bad debt relief.
BOX 6 Total of BOXES 4–5

BOX 7 BOX 3 less BOX 6
BOX 8 Sales plus exports less VAT Enter (A) + (B) + (C) less (H)
BOX 9 Purchases plus imports ENTER (D) + (F)

Note:
Boxes 1–3 are always amounts owed to H.M. Customs and Excise
Boxes 4–6 are always amounts owed by H.M. Customs and Excise

Value Added Tax Return

For the period
to

H M Customs and Excise — Due to reach the VAT Central Unit by
These dates must not be altered.

For Official Use

Registration No: 123 1234 12   Period: 02/87

Before you fill in this form please read the notes on the other side. You must complete all boxes — writing "none" where necessary. If you need to show an exact amount of pounds, please write "00" in the pence column. Don't put a dash or leave the column blank. Please write clearly in ink.
You must ensure that the completed form and any VAT payable are received no later than the due date by the Controller, VAT Central Unit, H M Customs and Excise, 21 Victoria Avenue, SOUTHEND-ON-SEA X

[SPECIMEN]

An envelope is enclosed for your use.

For Official Use

		£	p	
VAT DUE in this period on OUTPUTS (sales, etc), certain postal imports and services received from abroad	1	900	00	(H)
Underdeclarations of VAT made on previous returns (but not those notified in writing by Customs and Excise)	2	NONE		
TOTAL VAT DUE (box 1 + box 2)	3	900	00	
VAT DEDUCTIBLE in this period on INPUTS (purchases, etc)	4	515	00	(E) + (G)
Overdeclarations of VAT made on previous returns (but not those notified in writing by Customs and Excise)	5	NONE		
TOTAL VAT DEDUCTIBLE (box 4 + box 5)	6	515	00	
NET VAT PAYABLE OR REPAYABLE (Difference between boxes 3 and 6)	7	385	00	
Value of Outputs (excluding any VAT)	8	7700		(A) + (B) +
Value of Inputs (excluding any VAT)	9	5100		(D) + (F) −

FOR OFFICIAL USE

Please tick only ONE of these boxes:
- box 3 greater than box 6 — payment by credit transfer — payment enclosed
- box 6 greater than box 3 — repayment due

How to pay the VAT due
Cross all cheques and postal orders "A/C Payee only" and make them payable to "H M Customs and Excise". Make credit transfers through account 3078027 at National Girobank or 10-70-50 2055000 for Bank Giros and keep your payment slip. You can order pre-printed booklets of credit transfer slips from your local VAT office. In your own interest do not send notes, coins, or uncrossed postal orders through the post.
Please write your VAT registration number on the back of all cheques and credit transfer slips.

Please tick box(es) if the statement(s) apply:
- box 5 includes bad debt relief
- box 8 includes exempt outputs
- box 8 includes exports ✓

Retail schemes If you have used any of the schemes in the period covered by this return please tick the box(es) to show all the schemes used.

| A | B | C | D | E | F✓ | G | H | J |

Remember, you could be liable to a financial penalty if your return and all the VAT payable are not received by the due date.
DECLARATION by the signatory to be completed by or on behalf of the person named above.

I, ANDREW NEIL OTHER .... declare that the
(full name of signatory in BLOCK LETTERS)
information given above is true and complete.

Signed A N Other .... Date 29 February 1987

proprietor, partner, director, secretary, responsible officer, committee member of club or association, duly authorised person   *Delete as necessary

FOR OFFICIAL USE

F3790 (JULY 1986)

CHAPTER SIXTEEN

Your legal rights and obligations

There are a host of penalties for failures to comply with the requirements of the law on VAT. Some are *criminal* and as such offenders will face possible prosecution in the ordinary courts before magistrates or a judge. Others are *civil* and provide for a penalty to be paid in the event of a particular breach which is automatic unless certain things can be proved.

The civil penalties were introduced in the Finance Act 1985. Some did not take effect immediately. Some criminal offences have been superseded by the new provisions and have been repealed.

The law as it now stands is complex and its provisions may be devastating for the businessman. The automatic penalties could mean the difference between survival and failure in business due to their severe financial implications.

The current position is best put into table form to illustrate the law at a glance. (See tables A and B).

There are a number of non-duplication provisions for situations where an act may give rise to both criminal and civil actions or more than one civil action.

Now that a range of civil penalties are available to the Customs and Excise, *criminal* actions are likely to be brought by them in only the more serious of cases. The smaller business has certainly the most to fear from the effect of the *civil* penalties. Most are now in force with the exception of provisions for interest and the 'serious misdeclaration' penalty. Customs and Excise plan to introduce these later in 1989.

For the smaller enterprise it is perhaps penalties for mistakes that result in underpayment or overclaiming of VAT (serious misdeclaration) and the range of penalties available to Customs and Excise for failure to submit VAT returns and/or payments on time (default surcharge and breaches of regulatory provisions) that will cause the majority of problems. Also, for the unregistered and growing business there is the constant need to monitor turnover for registration requirements (see Chapter 2) to ensure no infringement is made that will incur a penalty for failure to notify and register which could be 30% of VAT due.

The serious misdeclaration penalty is planned to be introduced later in 1989 and although it will take a little time for its full effect to be felt, there is little room for complacency. It is essential to ensure now that your VAT accounting systems are in order and able to meet the legal requirements expected of them. On implementation, any underdeclaration or overclaim of VAT becomes subject to a possible penalty of 30% of the potential tax loss. You are given some leeway as regards the size of mistake you are allowed to make and with what frequency. A particularly dangerous element in the serious misdeclaration penalty is the obligation it places upon you to inform Customs and Excise if they raise an assessment that is less than the true amount of VAT due. If the difference exceeds the limits shown in the table you may trigger off a penalty by your failure to notify Customs and Excise of the difference. You will no longer, therefore, be able to successfully delay payment of the true amount of VAT due by simply paying assessments until a VAT officer visits you and discovers the difference. In any case, failures to submit timely returns and payments constitute civil breaches which also give rise to penalties.

In the case of failures to submit returns and/or payments of VAT on time, you now place yourself in the unenviable position of liability to more than one civil penalty. Although Customs and Excise can only impose one penalty they have the choice of that penalty. It is not unreasonable to expect them to choose that which in your case will achieve the largest financial penalty. (See default surcharge section later in this chapter and (c) & (d) section table B).

In the case of the default surcharge you are given two opportunities to be late in a twelve month period. After that you render yourself liable to penalties for further defaults made within the twelve months following notification by Customs and Excise of pending liability under the surcharge rules. Depending on the frequency of these failures the penalty may be as large as 30% of the outstanding tax.

Where Customs and Excise raise a penalty for breach of the appropriate regulatory provisions, you may either be subjected to a fixed daily penalty or a percentage of the VAT due whichever leads to the greater penalty. The fixed penalty may be as much as £30 per day for each day the failure continues, or $\frac{1}{2}$% of the tax due, depending on the frequency of the failure. Customs and Excise have named 40 regulations, breach of which will give rise to a civil penalty. The regulations are many and more may yet be identified. They range from rules concerning the content of a tax invoice to failure to notify partner details in a partnership.

The only 'defence' that can be offered for civil infringements is that of 'reasonable excuse'. This defence is available for all civil breaches with the exception of tax evasion (for which there is the morally questionable mitigable action of co-operation with Customs and Excise to reduce the potential penalty by half).

Tribunals have no general power to mitigate the set penalties. They may only find 'reasonable excuse' which becomes an absolute defence giving rise to no penalties. We are told by law that a reasonable excuse is not an inability to pay VAT due, nor is it applicable where the blame for the failure lies with a third party (eg your accountant or an employee). We are not told by law what may constitute a reasonable excuse and we must therefore look to the decisions of the Tribunals.

Customs and Excise have now issued some broad guidelines on their interpretations of a reasonable excuse. There are also a number of VAT tribunal case decisions, particularly concerning failure to register on time. To date virtually all of the penalties raised and appeals heard on the grounds of reasonable excuse have concerned failures to register. Very small businesses have therefore been the hardest hit by the civil penalty system. However, the principles in the cases are often relevant to other civil penalties. It must nevertheless be remembered that all cases of reasonable excuse will have different facts surrounding them and it will not necessarily follow that a reasonable excuse will be found in all cases with similar circumstances. So far there have been a number of inconsistencies in tribunal decisions which are often difficult to reconcile.

In general there might be a reasonable excuse in the following instances:

a Illness which prevents a small businessman complying with VAT requirements.

b Ignorance and inexperience where all the circumstances support the view that it is unreasonable to have expected a full understanding of requirements, eg as with young people with little experience or education to rely on. However there have been cases where such excuses have been specifically disallowed from constituting a reasonable excuse.

c Where a trader has done everything that could reasonably be expected of him to

Table A The criminal offences (unless otherwise indicated, the maximum penalty is that awarded summarily)

The offence	Notes on the offence	Maximum penalty	
FRAUDULENT EVASION	This applies to any person who is knowingly concerned in or takes steps with a view to evasion of VAT (includes the receipt of repayments by fraudulent means).	SUMMARY:	Greater of £2000 fine or 3 × tax evaded; or 6 months' imprisonment; or both.
		INDICTMENT:	Unlimited fine or 7 years' imprisonment or both.
DEALING IN FALSE DOCUMENTS	This applies to any person who, with intent to deceive, in any way makes use of a document which, with regard to VAT is false in material particular. This includes the production, furnishing, or sending of such a document or causing the same. Document could mean a VAT Return.	SUMMARY:	£2000 fine, or if the document is a required return or, a claim for refund of tax, a penalty of 3 × total tax avoided/claimed; or 6 months' imprisonment; or both
		INDICTMENT:	Unlimited fine or 7 years' imprisonment or both
MAKING FALSE STATEMENTS	This applies to any person making a Statement in the course of furnishing information he knows to be false in material particular, or is reckless in this regard.	SUMMARY:	£2000 fine or if the information is contained in or is otherwise relevant to a required return, a penalty of 3 × total tax avoided/claimed; or 6 months' imprisonment.
		INDICTMENT:	Unlimited fine or 7 years' imprisonment or both.
CONDUCT WHICH NECESSITATES AN OFFENCE	If a person's conduct must have involved one of the above three offences, then he is liable under this provision.	SUMMARY:	The greater of £2000 fine or 3 × tax intended to be evaded or imprisonment for 6 months or both.
		INDICTMENT:	Unlimited fine or imprisonment for 7 years or both.
SUPPORTING VAT EVASION	This is an act of receiving goods or services where there is reason to believe that tax has or will be evaded on them.		THE GREATER OF £2000 FINE OR 3 × TAX INVOLVED.

Table B The civil penalties

OFFENCE	CRITERIA	STATUTORY MAXIMUM PENALTY	STATUTORY DEFENCES AND MITIGATIONS	EFFECTIVE DATE
TAX EVASION (INCLUDES ATTEMPTS TO WRONGFULLY RECLAIM VAT)	There must be an element of dishonesty in what is done.	An amount equal to the tax evaded or sought to be evaded.	Co-operation with Customs and Excise in their investigation may reduce the penalty by half.	25 July 1985
SERIOUS MISDECLARATION OR NEGLECT RESULTING IN UNDERSTATEMENTS OR OVERCLAIMS	Liability to Tax is understated on a return, or underassessed where C&E are not informed within 30 days. Other conditions are: **a** Equals or exceeds 30% of the true tax, or **b** Equals or exceeds the greater of £10,000 and 5% of the true tax.	30% of the tax which would have been lost if the understatement had not been discovered.	There is a reasonable excuse for the conduct OR all information was furnished by you to C&E regarding the misdeclaration when you had no reason to believe you were subject to an investigation. Voluntary disclosures of errors will not count towards penalty if disclosure is made without the prompt of a forthcoming inspection visit from Customs and Excise.	Mid-1989
PERSISTENT MISDECLARATION	If errors are made on two or more VAT returns within a two year period a penalty may be charged if another error is made within a further two years. Errors must exceed £100 or 1% of the VAT due in a period. Unprompted voluntary disclosures will not contribute towards a penalty.	15% of the VAT involved.	Reasonable excuse.	

Table B *continued*

OFFENCE	CRITERIA	STATUTORY MAXIMUM PENALTY	STATUTORY DEFENCES AND MITIGATIONS	EFFECTIVE DATE
FAILURE TO: **a** KEEP RECORDS AS REQUIRED		£500.00		25 July 1985
b COMPLY WITH VAT REGULATIONS: NOTIFY CESSATION OF TAXABLE SUPPLIES* FURNISH INFORMATION AND PRODUCE DOCUMENTS*		The amount of penalty is determined by the number of other failures that have occurred in the 2 years prior to the beginning of the failure: | CATEGORY	NO. OF FAILURES	DAILY† PENALTIES £
---	---	---
I	NONE	5
II	ONE	10
III	OTHER	15		Reasonable excuse	25 July 1985

* These are only two examples of approximately forty regulations breach of which may give rise to these penalties.
† The daily penalty can be levied up to a maximum of 100 days.

Table B *continued*

OFFENCE	CRITERIA	STATUTORY MAXIMUM PENALTY	STATUTORY DEFENCES AND MITIGATIONS	EFFECTIVE DATE
c PAY VAT DUE ON TIME		The greater of: **a** As per above table **b** A fraction of tax due as per table below	Reasonable excuse	1 October 1986
d SUBMIT A VAT RETURN ON TIME		<table><tr><th>CATEGORY AS PER ABOVE TABLE</th><th>FRACTION TO BE APPLIED TO TAX DUE</th></tr><tr><td>I</td><td>$\frac{1}{6}$ of 1%</td></tr><tr><td>II</td><td>$\frac{1}{3}$ of 1%</td></tr><tr><td>III</td><td>$\frac{1}{2}$ of 1%</td></tr></table>		1 October 1986
FAILURE TO NOTIFY LIABILITY FOR REGISTRATION	This also includes failure to notify a change in the nature of supplies if there has been an exemption from registration.	30% of the VAT due or £50.00 if greater (or no VAT is due) The level of penalty depends on how late the notification is: Up to 9 months 10% 9–18 months 20% over 18 months 30%	Reasonable excuse	25 July 1985

Table B *continued*

OFFENCE	CRITERIA	STATUTORY MAXIMUM PENALTY	STATUTORY DEFENCES AND MITIGATIONS	EFFECTIVE DATE
UNAUTHORISED ISSUE OF A TAX INVOICE	– –	30% of the VAT wrongfully shown on the invoice or £50.00.	Reasonable excuse	25 July 1985
BREACHES OF WALKING POSSESSION	– –	Half of the VAT due	Reasonable excuse	25 July 1985

Note: A '*Reasonable excuse*' does **not** include:
  a Inability to pay tax due
  b The fact that the failure was due to your accountant or any third party

comply with VAT law. For example, if a trader submits VAT registration forms, hears nothing from Customs and Excise in return but periodically follows up the application. If Customs and Excise still fail to act he might have a reasonable excuse. It is now necessary to keep any evidence of follow ups, such as notes of telephone calls, copies of letters, etc.

d Where there are reasonable doubts as to whether a trader is employed or self employed and as a result of this confusion he fails to register for VAT.

The following have not been accepted as a reasonable excuse:

a Ignorance of the law in general.
b Failure to meet a VAT requirement because of business pressures.
c Errors in calculating turnover for registration purposes.
d No loss of VAT to Customs and Excise. For example, in cases where all a person's customers are VAT registered and would reclaim VAT charged to them by the defaulter anyway.

Interest penalties

Interest provisions will become effective in late 1989. Interest may be charged where Customs and Excise assess VAT due:

a Because a VAT return has not been submitted to them or payment of VAT due has not been made.
b Where Customs and Excise do not believe returns to be correct.
c Where a person fails to notify liability to register or notify changes in the nature of supplies made where he has been exempted from registration.
d Where VAT has been wrongly charged on an invoice by an unauthorised person.

The default surcharge

A default occurs if a return is not submitted or tax due on it is not paid on time. To incur a surcharge a default must occur twice within one year. Customs and Excise must then serve a '*surcharge liability notice*'. This gives a period within which a surcharge will be incurred on further default. This period is called the *surcharge period*. The surcharge period runs from the date of the surcharge liability notice to one year after the end of the second default VAT period. If a surcharge liability notice is issued which overlaps with another, the second notice is treated as an extension of the first, creating a longer, single surcharge period. The surcharge is a percentage of the outstanding VAT debt (see table below). The surcharge is £30 if that is a greater sum than the surcharge calculated by using the table.

A '*reasonable excuse*' for the default will prevent a surcharge being imposed and will wipe the default off the record for the purposes of the table.

Although the law does not specify what *will* constitute a reasonable excuse, the law does tell us what will *not*. It will *not* include:

a Your inability to pay the VAT at the time it was due.
b The fact that the failure was due to your accountant or a third party. This is a civil matter between you and that person.

There is a non-duplication provision in the event of a penalty having already been charged for the breach of the equivalent regulation, ie failure to render returns, or pay tax.

No penalty can be charged if you can prove that the VAT return and payment have been posted in good time to arrive by the date it is due. This is because Customs and Excise are effectively using the Post Office as their agents. Penalty does not therefore depend on receipt of the VAT return by Customs and Excise. It is therefore prudent to

Default surcharge table

PERIOD	% TO APPLY TO OUTSTANDING TAX
1st Default in Surcharge Period	5
2nd	10
3rd	15
4th	20
5th	25
6th	30
All subsequent Defaults in Surcharge Period	30

obtain certificates of posting from the post office and keep any other notes that may support a claim of posting, eg notes of the person posting it, where and when. A certificate will generally act as suitable evidence to prove posting in the event of a dispute.

Power of Customs and Excise to seize and take samples of goods

Customs and Excise have the power to remove samples if it seems necessary for the protection of the Revenue. Items removed must be returned within a reasonable time and in reasonably the same state. Failure to do this results in a right to compensation.

Power of Customs and Excise to enter and search

Customs and Excise may use this power at reasonable times for the purpose of enforcing VAT laws. In practice, senior officials will organise such manoeuvres and issue instructions unless the situation is one of extreme urgency.

More probably, a warrant will have been sought from a Justice of the Peace, who must be satisfied that a fraud offence has been or soon will be committed. The warrant lasts for 14 days and allows reasonable seizure of goods and documents for evidence. It also provides for the physical search of persons. A female can only be searched by another female.

Power to inspect computers

This power covers the right to inspect, at any reasonable time, the operation of any computer and associated apparatus, which is or has been used in connection with the business accounts. Customs and Excise may require any computer operator or similar employee to give assistance in the inspection.

Customs and Excise power to open gaming machines

An officer may require a person to open his gaming machine at any reasonable time and account for the takings inside it. This is to give Customs and Excise access to knowledge regarding expected take as otherwise this form of cash take would be impossible to gauge.

Liaison of Customs and Excise with the Inland Revenue

This is often a cause of considerable concern to traders, especially those who are assessed for reasons that might also affect their liability to pay other taxes, eg income tax, corporation tax and capital gains tax. This commonly happens where sales are discovered to be underdeclared. The law does provide for the exchange of information between Customs and Excise and the Inland Revenue. However, this is believed to be used infrequently and only in cases where considerable sums of money are involved. There have been recent liaison experiments and closer liaison could well be a feature of future tax control.

Assessments

Assessments may be raised in a number of different circumstances:
a   In the absence of a VAT return.
b   Where an under-declaration of tax is revealed.
c   Where civil penalties are charged.
d   Where interest or a default surcharge is charged.

The infringement must be assessable and the assessment itself must be made within a certain time limit dating from either:
a   The event giving rise to the infringement.
or
b   The accounting period within which the infringement was made.
or
c   The death of the person.

The time limits themselves vary, according to the infringement, from 3 years following a death, to 20 years for fraud. A period of 6 years applies to most infringements.

The general rule is that an assessment cannot be made after the later of
a   two years after the end of the accounting period concerned;
b   one year after Customs and Excise have had knowledge or sufficient evidence to make an assessment, with a maximum of six years after the accounting period.

The sums assessed should be allocated, by Customs and Excise, as closely as possible to respective VAT periods. If you receive an assessment it is wise to investigate the time limit that applies to your circumstances and ensure the assessment has been made within it.

If you cannot pay your VAT

Debt recovery

We will now look at the situation if you do not pay your VAT and how it is recovered by the Customs and Excise. Bankruptcy and liquidation are usually last resorts. If you find yourself in this position you will be at the mercy of the ordinary law on the subject. These are large subjects and outside the scope of this book. However, do note, that debts for VAT due to Customs and Excise have certain preferences over any other creditors. Any VAT due at the time of the legal proceedings (eg date of receiving order, death of debtor, date of winding up order, appointment of liquidator), which has become due within the twelve month period before that date is a *preferential* debt. It has rights above the claims of ordinary creditors. if the VAT due stems from a period previous to the twelve month period, the VAT ranks alongside the ordinary creditors:

The usual sequence of events in recovery of VAT due is as follows:
a   You are contacted (usually by telephone) to ensure that you have not forwarded payment which has, in error, not been recorded by Customs and Excise.

b If it is ascertained that you have not forwarded payment you will receive a letter demanding immediate payment on threat of 'distraint' (this is explained below).

At this point you are well advised to consider applying for time to pay if you have not already done so. You should write to a more senior official (see page 109) of the local VAT office. Set out your problems over payment and state how you propose to pay the tax due that is in arrears, together with the tax that accumulates every period. You are best advised to enclose a down payment and propose that the balance be paid over a period of say six months. If you can convince Customs and Excise that your problems will clear up, this will strengthen your case, eg you have secure contracts in the pipeline; you are clearing non-recurring expenses, etc. The granting of time to pay is not a right, but a discretion which Customs and Excise operate in extenuating circumstances. Remember failure to pay VAT due on time may give rise to a civil penalty (see Table B page 98).

Distraint

Failure to pay

If you cannot pay your VAT and no extension of time to pay is granted, Customs and Excise may resort to the *levying of distress*.

This involves selecting items of your property for sale by public auction to recover both the amount of VAT owing and fees incurred in making the levy.

Distress will only be levied after the expiration of 30 days after the tax becomes due, and after a demand for it has been made.

Without prior warning, you will be called on by an officer of Customs and Excise who will be accompanied by a certified bailiff. The bailiff is there mainly to advise on the value of goods.

You will be asked whether you have submitted payment recently; if you have you will be requested to supply details of it, eg cheque number and date. Failing this you will be asked to immediately pay the amount due. The amount due will be shown on a distress warrant in the possession of the officer. More VAT may be due than that shown on the warrant, but distress can only be levied to the sum on the warrant. The warrant will be shown to you on request. It is signed by a higher official at the VAT office. It authorises the officials named to levy distress on the goods and chattels of the person named on the warrant, to the extent of the sum stated on the warrant.

It is unlikely that Customs and Excise will levy distress unless they see a responsible person of the business. So you often get a reprieve if neither you nor a responsible person is available for interview when the officer calls.

If distress is levied the items will be listed on a form of which you get a copy. Sufficient items are chosen to cover the debt if they are to be sold at a public auction. Arrangements may be made for their immediate removal from your premises to a place of storage. More likely an agreement will be entered into with you that you will not interfere with (eg sell or use) the goods for a certain period of time, after which they will be removed for sale. Breach of such an agreement may lead to a civil penalty (see Table B page 98).

Either way, sale can only be made five days or more after the date of the distraint. If you pay the debt and costs of the levy (see below) in this period, the goods will be restored to you. This gives you a period of extra grace for you to pay or re-apply to Customs and Excise for time to pay.

Costs

Costs of levying distress were once the subject of dispute. It is now settled by the Finance Act 1984 that you are liable for costs after 21 July 1984. Customs and Excise charged and collected costs of distress prior to 14 January 1984. These are now recoverable by traders who paid them, on application to the Customs and Excise.

You are liable for the fees the bailiff charges for levying distress, even if the items are not eventually removed and sold. These fees are calculated as a percentage of the debt. You are also liable for any other costs involved in removing and selling the goods, or maintaining a man on your premises to keep watch on the items to ensure they are not interfered with.

What items can be distrained upon

The goods and chattels distrained upon must be the property of the VAT registered entity. Hence items on lease or HP cannot be distrained upon, nor can land. Remember, if you feel that you have been treated unfairly in any way, you may have recourse to the courts.

The law protecting you from the abuse of powers held by authorities

This is a large legal subject which cannot be fully developed within the present work. In many areas the law remains unsettled, and there often seems room for new situations and amendments to existing legal decisions. We aim to draw your attention to the areas in which the Courts have been known to interfere. The Customs and Excise have many powers under the VAT Act 1983 and subsequent Finance Acts and Statutory Instruments. This does not mean that they cannot be questioned by the Courts. The Customs and Excise cannot just claim 'We have the power!'

Over many years the Courts have developed a set of principles by which all authorities are bound. These give protection to those affected by decisions of authorities. A statute may exclude or incorporate some of the detailed rules of law in its creation; but the Courts construe such exclusions with the greatest severity to prevent injustices. Frequently the Courts have found new ways in which to avoid the strict wording of a statute or to imply these rules where the statute is silent.

Each case turns on its individual facts. If you feel that you may have a case because your situation fits within the following principles, you *must* consult your solicitor. He will advise you, both as to whether you have a case, and whether it is worth pursuing.

You may have a right under the following principles to apply for what is called 'judicial review', under *Rule 55 Rules of the Supreme Court*. This means that the High Court, Queen's Bench Division, will examine the decision of the authority. It may decide to make an order that affects the decision. The orders may take three forms:

a   An order to quash the decision (technically called 'certiorari').
b   An order that the case be heard by the authority (technically called 'mandamus').
c   An order to prevent the case being heard by the authority (technically called 'prohibition').

Before going further we ask you to note the consequences of commencing an action. To succeed in the High Court will involve instructing both a solicitor and a barrister.

Should the action be unsuccessful you will probably bear all the costs—both your own and those of the Customs and Excise. This could be in the region of £5,000. An appeal to the Court of Appeal might cost circa £10,000 in total.

The court has what is known as an 'equitable discretion' as to whether it will make an order. It will look at your conduct. This includes having regard to any delay in bringing the action and untruthfulness on your part at any stage of the case. Even if you obtain an order, the Court could penalise you for bad conduct by refusing to award you costs.

The rules below apply to 'the Authority'. Some will be appropriate to an individual officer making a decision, some only to a decision by a VAT Tribunal (see Chapter 17). As a general rule, situations I and II below may apply to both, whereas situation III only to a Tribunal. Situation I will apply to all acts of the Customs and Excise. Situation II may only apply to the discretion of an individual officer where he is under a duty to use that discretion 'judicially', ie as if he were a court himself.

SITUATION I: Where the Authority exceeds the powers conferred by statute (technically called *ultra vires*).

This may happen if the Authority acts outside the powers given it by statute. Customs and Excise have no power to do as much as breathe except where statute allows it. The power may not exist at all; or it may be delegated to a lower ranking official not specified by statute.

SITUATION II: Where the authority abuses a discretion it is given by the law.

Any power conferred upon an authority to decide upon something must be exercised 'lawfully', ie the authority must not:
a ignore relevant considerations;
b take notice of irrelevant considerations;
c act for improper purposes (ie a power is given for a certain purpose and it cannot be used for any other—this is very similar to situation I);
d fetter their discretion (eg by unreasonably following a policy or rule which has no statutory authority);
e act unreasonably (eg an official must not act in a way in which any other such official would not).

For example: Two retailers in the same street sell video films. They are entirely unconnected. The Customs and Excise discover fraudulent conduct in the first. The second receives an assessment which is higher and appears based solely on the facts of the other retailer. The second may appeal to a VAT Tribunal which must take these matters into account. Otherwise, Customs and Excise would be exercising improper consideration.

SITUATION III: 'natural justice'. Many of the principles of natural justice have been expressly incorporated into the rules of the VAT Tribunal by Statutory Instrument (see Chapter 16). They and others are summarized below:

An authority must:
a Hear your side of the case. This means it must give you:
   i   'Prior notice of any proceedings' to enable you to prepare your case (fixed at least 14 days before the hearing date).
   ii knowledge of the charge. As you will have initiated the appeal you will know the issues involved. You are also given the right to obtain some of the documentary evidence. Customs and Excise hold against you (see p. 112).

    iii   time to prepare your case.

There are strict time limits (see Chapter 16) which may be extended by agreement but not as of right.

If a case is unusually complex and involves considerable work, for instance by professional lawyers and accountants, a court may feel strict adherence to time limits to be unreasonable.

    iv   A hearing (see p. 110).
    v   A right to call witnesses (see pp. 112–113).
    vi   A right to cross examine hostile witnesses (see pp. 112–113).
    vii   A right to representation—legal or otherwise (see p. 114).
    viii   A right to have reasons given for a decision. These must be recorded and a signed statement sent to you. This must contain all findings of fact and reasons for the decision.

b   Not to be biased.

Bias can take many and varied forms:

    i   A pecuniary bias, eg a financial interest in the decision being made in a certain way;
    ii   A bias in favour of friends or relatives;
    iii   A bias because the person making the decision effectively acts as both the prosecutor and the judge.

In many cases simply the outward appearance of bias may suffice to lead the Courts to make an order. Lawyers quote a well known phrase of Lord Hewart C.J. in R. v Sussex Justices ex parte McCarthy (1924): 'Justice must not only be done, but should manifestly and undoubtedly be seen to be done.'

However, on a more sad note, even if you should succeed in obtaining an order from the High Court quashing a decision, the Court will often order the decision to be made again—this time properly. It then seems that the Tribunals will give the same *decision* as before but with *correct reasons*.

Finally, do remember that the High Court will expect you to have exhausted all possible internal reviews by Customs and Excise before you enter their courtrooms.

The Ombudsman (The Parliamentary Commissioner For Administration)

This official is given the power to inquire into the conduct of authorities in the course of their administration of Acts of Parliament. His actual powers do not allow him to change a decision but his reports carry great persuasive power.

He has a discretion to review cases of 'maladministration'. This is not defined, although cases in the courts have seen the judges offer definitions and give examples of maladministration. It could include bias, neglect, delay, incompetence, arbitrariness, etc. Misleading statements by an official have been held to be acts of maladministration.

If you feel you have suffered an act of maladministration you can complain via your MP to the Ombudsman. Your MP need not refer the case. Your case will probably only receive attention if you have been either grossly aggrieved in such circumstances as deny you legal redress, or where several cases are brought to his attention, forming a pattern in a particular geographical area. If you have a good case for complaint this is an avenue well worth pursuing to achieve results. The Ombudsman has already examined a number of Customs and Excise VAT cases.

CHAPTER SEVENTEEN

Using the Tribunal

General

Tribunals are intended to provide an uncomplicated and flexible court structure where certain decisions that have been made by Customs and Excise can be reviewed and judged by an impartial body. The aim is to steer away from the expense involved in going to the ordinary courts of law. In many cases you will be able to represent yourself at a tribunal without engaging qualified lawyers. However, the Tribunals are becoming more 'legalistic' in their approach with the passing of time and the ever increasing legal complexities that arise. If you are not satisfied with the eventual decisions of the tribunal, there is provision in some cases for appeal to the ordinary courts. Tribunals must have regard to certain principles of law, as must other public authorities. If they are in breach of these principles you may be able to get a decision reviewed by the ordinary courts. These principles of law are discussed on pages 106–108. Furthermore a Committee has been set up to act as a watchdog over certain tribunals to ensure that they act in accordance with an Act of Parliament, namely The Tribunals and Inquiries Act. This Act lays down certain standards for most tribunals including VAT Tribunals, eg tribunals must give reasons for their decisions.

We hope to guide you through the VAT Tribunal system in order that you may have the confidence to use it if the need should ever arise.

Before hastily leaping to a Tribunal

Tribunals are very expensive for the Customs and Excise and they often prefer to reconsider a decision made by an officer at a more senior level. You are well advised to ask Customs and Excise to review your case before heading straight to a VAT Tribunal. You must prepare your case well at this stage as if you were going to the Tribunal. A changed decision by review will save you time, money and concern.

You must also act promptly in asking for a review as there are time limits within which an appeal to a tribunal must be served after Customs and Excise have officially notified you of their decision.

The time limit is 30 days after the date of the letter from Customs and Excise to you containing their decision.

Customs and Excise may extend this if they are reviewing your case. You should obtain this fact in writing from them.

The Tribunal can also extend the time limit on application. They can also decide to hear an appeal if the time limit has been exceeded. However, do not rely on this and let time lapse without obtaining some official extension.

Who to ask in Customs and Excise for a review

As is usual with civil service departments there is a ladder of authority. This is explained in Chapter 1. See who has signed the letter containing the decision and ask his rank. Then write to the local VAT office asking for a review (quickly) by the next person(s) a rank or two up the ladder. You could always go to the top of the local tree to raise attention to your case. In your letter you are advised to state that you wish to appeal to a VAT Tribunal but request to have a local review first of all.

Preparing your case to present to Customs and Excise

This must be taken seriously. A well prepared case may make Customs and Excise change their decision and avoid a tribunal hearing.

Prepare it as if you were doing so for the Tribunal. Obviously, each case will rest on its individual merit and we cannot prepare examples for every case that may come up.

However, there are some cases that are very common with similarities in the way Customs and Excise decide them and the ways in which you may defend them. For example, Customs and Excise make a lot of VAT assessments on takings not declared by retailers. They examine retailers' accounts, bearing in mind the profit margins they would expect from similar businesses. If they receive no convincing explanation why your margins are less, they may assess what they think your takings ought to be, by applying profit percentages to your purchases. This is only in broad outline. There are defences you can raise. An example of a case against a retailer, with an appropriate 'defence' is shown on page 115.

We must now look at the Tribunal system:

Can you appeal to a VAT tribunal?

Before going through the rules of procedure on appeals to VAT Tribunals, you must know whether or not your case is one which can be heard by this body. VAT Tribunals can only hear cases about certain things. We shall list the more common ones for you. There are many more which are not so common. If you are unsure whether your case is one for which you may appeal, contact the Tribunal without delay. Tribunal staff are usually very helpful over matters of procedure.

Where an appeal lies to a VAT Tribunal.

a   Where you are registered or deregistered.
b   Where relief for input tax is disallowed.
c   Where VAT is decided to be chargeable on a supply you make.
d   Where you are assessed for VAT due.
e   Where bad debt relief is refused.
f   Where liability to a penalty or surcharge is in dispute.

Note that a Tribunal can only reduce the amount of a penalty as prescribed by law. It may thus reduce any penalty for tax evasion or conduct involving dishonesty, to half, depending on the extent to which the offender has co-operated. Otherwise Tribunals are unable to mitigate the amount of penalty.

There are further conditions to be met before you can appeal namely:

i   All VAT returns must have been completed and sent in.
ii All amounts of VAT due must have been paid over by you. This includes any tax due from an assessment which you are now appealing against.

Number **ii** above could lead to a very unfair situation if you are disputing an amount of tax Customs and Excise say is due and your case is justified and later held correct. Therefore concessions may be made. Either Customs and Excise or the Tribunal may allow an appeal to be heard without payment of VAT due if they feel that to pay would cause 'hardship'. So, if you cannot pay, you must quickly apply for this concession (remember the time limits).

Note: payments of civil penalties, interest or surcharges do not have to be made before an appeal is heard.

How you appeal for dispensation from ii

a   By approaching the Customs and Excise
This is the first step—approach the department before rushing into the Tribunal.
Address your letter to a senior official (see Chapter 1) for guidance). You must prove that if you have to pay the VAT before the appeal is heard this would cause hardship, eg your business would suffer badly. You will hope to prove this, eg by showing evidence of your funds and of your business commitments.

b   By approaching the Tribunal
You will need to prove to the Tribunal's satisfaction the same hardship grounds as those which form the basis of an approach to Customs and Excise (see above).
You must have your application heard by the Tribunal. Procedures are virtually the same as for the hearing of an appeal against the disputed decision itself. You must act promptly (remember the time limits).
You will eventually receive a statement of the case against your application by Customs and Excise. This will include any appropriate supporting documents. You will have to supply similar supporting documents to the Tribunal. Make sure you keep in regular contact with the tribunal officials dealing with your case, who can advise you if you are not sure of the next step.
You will be notified of the place, date, and time of the hearing. These sort of hearings are usually held in private, so details of your financial circumstances will not be made publicly available.

Appealing against the decision

By this stage you should have
a   considered an internal review by Customs and Excise;
b   have paid the VAT due, or arranged not to pay until after the Tribunal hearing as discussed above;
c   have submitted all VAT returns due to date.

We are now in a position to consider all the procedures you have to go through before the Tribunal will hear your case against the decision of Customs and Excise.
There are three different categories of appeal to which different time limits apply. These are:
a   appeals against tax evasion.
b   appeals for mitigation and reasonable excuse.
c   other appeals.

Stage I—*Notice of Appeal*
You must 'Serve a *Notice of Appeal*'.
A standard form is provided for this purpose (Trib. 1) and may be obtained from the Tribunal or from VAT offices. The form is quite self-explanatory.
Service is a legal requirement and takes effect from the date the Tribunal *receives* the form.
Remember too, the time limits. Service must, unless an extension is granted, be

made within 30 days of the date the disputed decision is formally given to you (ie the date of the letter from Customs and Excise which has their final decision in it).

You may apply to have your case heard at a tribunal centre other than the one usually considered the centre for your area. Obviously this may be worth considering if your tribunal centre is quite some distance from you. Again a standard form is made available for this purpose (Trib. 5).

If this application is granted all your subsequent dealings will be with the new centre.

You will always receive an acknowledgement for the receipt of your correspondence. Because of the time limits you must keep a check on the dates and how things are progressing. It may be a good idea to send correspondence by registered post or recorded delivery. This shows good faith on your part should there by any slip ups, and may strengthen your position. Keep pressure on the Tribunal centre if you think too much time has elapsed since your last letter.

Time limits are usually extended, in practice, but you must not be lulled into a false sense of security by this. The time limits are legal requirements and as such may be enforced.

Stage 2—*Documents*

You must list (within 30 days of service of the Notice of Appeal—or 15 days after the last day for Customs and Excise's reply in the case of a civil penalty for tax evasion), all documents you intend to use as evidence to support your case when you appear before the Tribunal. A form is supplied for this purpose which should be completed and forwarded on to the Tribunal within the time limit. The documents should be made available for Customs and Excise to inspect within seven to fourteen days after the date on the list. Customs and Excise are obliged to go through the same procedure for you.

A list of documents is not required in the case of appeals for mitigation and reasonable excuse.

Stage 3—*Stating the case*

Customs and Excise must serve a statement of the case (except where the appeal is one against civil penalty on the grounds of reasonable excuse or mitigation) to the Tribunal within 30 days of their being served notice of appeal or 42 days where the appeal is against a civil penalty for tax evasion. In the latter instance you are obliged to serve your defence within 42 days and the Customs and Excise reply to it must be within 21 days.

Stage 4—*Witnesses*

You may call witnesses at a tribunal hearing. Witnesses can be compelled by the Tribunal to attend on threat of a fine. To compel a witness to appear you must apply to the Tribunal. Again a standard form is made available for this purpose (Trib. 5).

If the Tribunal grants this application, you will be sent the summons and will have to serve it, or arrange for someone else to serve it. There are professional firms who will do this, eg firms of certified bailiffs. These may be found in the Yellow Pages of telephone directories. If you decide to serve the summons on the witness yourself, you must do it in a certain way: Give a copy of the summons (the court send you an original and copies), to the witness whilst showing him the original at the same time. There is a limit of four days before the date of the hearing within which the summons cannot be served. Witnesses may appeal to the Tribunal to get the summons revoked so they do not have to appear. If they do have to appear they are entitled to payment for expenses they incur as a result.

However, there is an alternative to getting a witness to make a personal appearance at the Tribunal to give evidence. A *witness statement* can be made by the witness and this may be produced to the Tribunal as evidence to support your case. A standard form is provided for the witness to make his statement (Trib. 3). The witness statement must be served within 21 days of the date of service of Customs and Excise case, or within 21 days of service of the notice of appeal in the case of *mitigation* and *reasonable excuse appeals*. Where the appeal is against an assessment to a civil penalty for tax evasion the 21 day time limit runs from the last date for Customs and Excise's service of their reply to the defence.

Either Customs and Excise or yourself can object (within 14 days after the date of service of the witness statement) to the witness statements on the grounds you want the witness to *appear*, or that the facts in the statement are not correct. Again, a standard form to object is available (Trib. 4). If this is accepted by the Tribunal, the witness may be compelled to make a personal appearance.

Stage 5—*You've got to the Tribunal*
You will have now dealt with all the necessary administrative procedures to enable you to set foot before the Tribunal.

Customs and Excise will be prepared to agree outside of the Tribunal hearing at this stage. If you do come to an agreement, the agreement is binding as if the Tribunal had determined the appeal as per the agreement in its entirety. However, an appellant may still pull out of such an agreement within 30 days of it. The agreement must be in writing.

More about the Tribunal

Before we go into the procedures involved in the actual tribunal hearing (which are not very involved at all) it is helpful to describe the workings of the Tribunal machinery in more detail.

a *Who sits on it?*
There are usually three people, including a chairman. The chairman announces the decision and he may hear some cases alone.

b *Who is it responsible to?*
By Act of Parliament the VAT Tribunals are under the supervision of the Council on Tribunals. They may consider and report on any matter which may be referred to the Council. To ensure its independence, there is no link between the Council, or the Tribunal, and Customs and Excise. By more general rule of law the Tribunal is responsible to the higher ordinary courts.

c *Can the public listen to a Tribunal hearing?*
Tribunal hearings are in public, unless the Tribunal otherwise directs. The Tribunal may direct for a hearing to be in private if you apply for it. This can be done on the standard form (Trib. 5).

Preliminary hearings to decide whether or not you can have a hearing before a Tribunal without paying the VAT due, are in private.

d *What evidence can be used at the Tribunal hearing?*
The ordinary courts of law have special rules about evidence that can be produced at

hearings. Tribunals are not so affected by such rules of evidence. It is up to the Tribunal whether or not it decides to admit or refuse evidence which you, or Customs and Excise, intend to produce. Both parties will have to produce the documents which have been listed and make them available to the other side for inspection.

If the Tribunal refuses to accept evidence, or you feel evidence is unfairly allowed, you may be able to have the Tribunal's decision set aside by the ordinary courts of law. One now gets involved in more complex legal matters. If you find yourself in this situation professional legal advice must be sought.

e *Do I need a lawyer to represent me at a Tribunal?*
You do not have to be legally represented at a hearing before a Tribunal. If points of law are involved, eg over the liability of transaction, it may be best to have legal advice, and possibly representation.

However, in the other matters, for example involving an assessment of VAT underdeclared on the basis of underdeclared sales etc, it may be best to represent yourself, using the guidelines in this chapter. (A specimen case preparation follows.)

You can be represented at a Tribunal by a friend or your accountant. In many cases, the latter may be of more use than a solicitor.

Remember, the idea of the VAT Tribunal system is to provide a more flexible body to hear your case and to replace the need for resort to the more formal ordinary courts.

f *If I appeal to a Tribunal and do not win, can the Tribunal increase the amount of VAT due?*
The Tribunal may increase an assessment of VAT made by Customs and Excise to the correct amount of tax due in cases where there has been an understatement of VAT due on a Return.

g *Can the Tribunal fine me in any way as an ordinary court might do?*
Failure to comply with a direction of the Tribunal gives the Tribunal power to fine an offender a maximum of £1,000.

Procedures at the Tribunal hearing

As has been constantly stressed, Tribunals are now snowed under with legal procedural requirements that affect you.

What if one party does not turn up to the Tribunal hearing?
The Tribunal can still carry on and hear the appeal. If you fail to appear, you may still apply to the Tribunal for a re-hearing (use the standard form Trib. 5 and make sure it is received by the Tribunal within 14 days of the date of the decision).

Who presents their case first?
In most cases it is your right to present your case to the Tribunal first, but this is not a requirement and Customs and Excise may present their case first if you wish. How you then present your case is in your own hands.

If the appeal is against a civil penalty for tax evasion Customs and Excise must present their case first as the burden of proof is theirs to show you acted dishonestly.

What about witnesses?
You can call these to support your case and can cross-examine them. The Tribunal has the power to direct a witness to swear on oath or the equivalent. It can also compel the attendance of a witness.

The Tribunal decision
After you have both presented your case, the Tribunal will make its decision, and often give it there and then. It may, on the other hand, wait and inform you of the decision by letter at a later date.
　　Decisions are made by a majority. The Chairman has a casting vote if there exists a stalemate situation, when he sits with only *one* other member.

Final matters to be dealt with at the Tribunal hearing
Costs: Either you or Customs and Excise may ask the Tribunal costs to be awarded against the other party. You will have to say how much you want to be awarded in the way of costs. If the Tribunal cannot reach a decision, it may refer the matter to another body for decision. You must be able to produce supporting evidence to show how you arrive at the figure for costs.
　　Customs and Excise do not generally ask for costs unless a very unmeritorious case has been brought and it is felt the case should not therefore be public funded.

Legal Aid
This is not available for VAT tribunal cases, although some legal advice may be obtained through a scheme known as the *Green Form Scheme* administered by most firms of solicitors.

Interest lost on pre-hearing tax payments
If you win your case, you may have lost interest on tax which you have to pay before the Tribunal would hear the case. This may justify an award of interest.
　　You must explain to the Tribunal how you think a fair rate of interest ought to be arrived at and provide evidence in support (eg current bank interest rates). In the same way interest could be awarded against you, eg if you lose the case and have not paid the VAT before the hearing because you obtained special dispensation.

Case study of an assessment and a defence
As we have already said, each case is individual in character and therefore it is not possible to examine all methods of presenting a case. However, some types of case repeatedly come up before Tribunals, or are subject to an assessment by Customs and Excise which may be *internally reviewed* by them (see page 109).
　　These cases are concerned with disputes over gross takings, records kept by retailers, eg shops, pubs and clubs. The typical case involves Customs and Excise officers checking the books and records of a retailer, and concluding that the record of your gross takings which has been used to calculate VAT due is both incorrect and understated. The officers then proceed to assess what they believe should be the correct figure for gross takings. They will then recalculate the VAT due on the basis of their gross takings assessment. If you cannot offer an acceptable explanation for any differences you may have little alternative other than to pay the extra VAT assessed.
　　The methods used by Customs and Excise to assess what your gross takings should be usually follow certain patterns, whatever sort of retailer you are. Likewise, there are similar defences you can offer against such assessments. We will show you how Customs and Excise may make a gross taking assessment, and how you may offer a defence, either before a Tribunal or in an internal review by Customs and Excise.
　　We will take the case of a Mr Beer who runs a public house. His main trading activities in the pub are:
a　Sales of pub drinks.
b　Off-licence sales of drinks.
c　Some bar snacks.

d Cigarettes.
e Some confectionery sales.
f Takings from gaming and amusement machines.

He is visited by officers of Customs and Excise, who decide to inspect his accounts in greater detail with a view to a possible assessment of gross takings and undeclared VAT. We shall firstly describe the likely ways in which this may be done.

Method 1—*Questioning*

You may be questioned to establish how and why there appears to be an underdeclaration of takings, and therefore VAT, and to discover by what amount there has been an underdeclaration. This would be the cheapest and quickest method by which Customs and Excise could make an assessment. Typical questions are as follows:

a Who has control over the till?
b Who checks off cash in the till against the till rolls?
c If there is a discrepancy, what figure is recorded in the accounts, ie cash in the till or the amount on the till rolls?
d Who records the gross takings in the accounts?
e Are bills paid in cash extracted from the till without allowing for this in the records of gross takings? If so, how much money is involved?
f Do you take stock for your own use? If so, do you account for the value (at cost) in the gross takings records? If not—how much money is involved?
g Do you take money out of the till for personal living expenses, etc. without recording these amounts as takings?

Method 2—*The Bank*

The money paid into your bank account may be checked over a period to see if this is greater than the amount of gross takings recorded. (Allowances may also be made for living expenses drawn from the till.) If it is greater, Customs and Excise may assess on this basis, assuming that the extra cash banked represents gross takings unrecorded.

To disprove this, you will have to show that the money paid into your bank account which exceeds your recorded gross takings (allowing for cash drawings if appropriate), reflects receipts other than those liable to VAT, eg loan transactions, gambling winnings, safe-keeping of money for friends and relations, etc.

Note: Your personal bank statements cannot be *demanded* by the Customs and Excise, only requested. However, Customs and Excise can apply to the court for bank statements to be produced if they have reasonable grounds for doing so.

Method 3—*Comparisons with annual accounts*

This involves a comparison of sales shown by the annual accounts produced by your accountant, with sales (usually net of VAT) as per your VAT accounts and returns, for similar periods of time. This can give rise to difficulties if there is a difference.

However, your accountant could supply a reason for this, other than underdeclared gross takings. Also, the annual accounts may not be correct. You will have to satisfy Customs and Excise that this was the case, perhaps by the submission of revised annual accounts to the Inland Revenue.

Method 4—*Profit percentages*

This involves estimating what your takings should have been in a period, by applying an average profit percentage to your purchases of stock. This is a method frequently used by Customs and Excise to assess retailers. In its simplest form the percentage may be agreed with you. More likely a full exercise will be undertaken to calculate the percentage more accurately. Typically this is done by establishing current percentage profits ('mark ups') on main selling lines.

This can be done by taking your current purchase prices of stock and comparing them with your current sales prices.

In Mr Beer's case, bottles of spirits and kegs of beer would have their sales prices calculated by

number of tots in bottle/pints of keg × price of tot/pint.

Example of mark up calculation:

Selling price = 50p

Purchase price = 30p

Mark up percentage on the product $= \dfrac{50-30}{30} \times \dfrac{100}{1} = 67\%$ mark up on purchases.

Account must then be taken of the pattern of purchasing. This is usually achieved by taking a sample trading period and estimating the cost of all purchases of the products for which you have calculated mark ups. A table can be drawn up, and from it a 'weighted average mark up' obtained. Commonly this will be applied to all your purchases of stock to obtain an overall sales figure.

Item	A Purchase price £	B Selling price £	C % Mark up	D Gross purchases in sample period £	E Gross selling price (C × D) + D £
X	1.00	1.50	50%	1,000	1,500
Y	2.00	2.50	25%	2,000	2,500
Totals				3,000	4,000

Average weighted mark up $= \dfrac{(E-D)}{D} \times 100\% = \dfrac{(4,000 - 3,000)}{3,000} \times 100\% = 33\tfrac{1}{3}\%$

This means of arriving at sales can be extended to cope with virtually all things sold. However, there are problems in arriving at mark ups due to the time factor of conducting such an exercise.

We shall now assume that Mr Beer has been assessed on estimated sales, calculated in the way described above, and wants to defend himself against the assessment. Let us look at the different ways in which he can do this. Of course, he must be able to produce some evidence to support his argument. He can submit the following arguments.

a *There are lower mark ups on some sales:*
He could maintain that Customs and Excise have not included items which have very low mark ups and materially affect the calculated average mark up. In Mr Beer's case he would want to make sure cigarettes are included in the calculations. They have comparatively low mark ups and command high prices—often a significant percentage of total turnover.

b *Representative weighting*
The period chosen to extract gross purchases of the items must be representative of average trading, eg seasonal fluctuations may exist with a greater incidence of sales with high or low mark up.

c *Non-comparable past and current mark ups*
Current mark ups are often assumed to be the same as those in the past. This may not be so. They may now be higher due to disproportionate inflationary increases of overhead expenses.

d *Price reductions*
Prices may have been reduced from time to time to stimulate trade.

e *Stock increases:*
If there have been stock increases during the period covered by the assessment, these must be accounted for. The increase in stocks will not have been sold and their sale value cannot therefore be reflected in gross takings, nor can VAT be due.

f *Theft of stock*
If it can be proved that stock has been stolen, this must be taken into account. In assessing gross takings VAT will not be due on stolen *stock*. However, VAT is due on stolen *takings*. Legally the supply has already been made and output tax is therefore due on the sale.

g *Alternative sale outlets for the same stock*
In the case of Mr Beer some stock is sold through an 'off-licence'. The mark up on this stock will be different—most likely lower than on bar sales. This should be accounted for in establishing the average mark up.

h *Losses of stock through wastage, damage, etc.*
In our example we can consider under this heading:
i   Spillage of beers.
ii Drips from spirits bottles or taps.
iii Breakages of bottles.
iv Drawing off beers before lunch or evening trade. Long feed lines.
v   Bad stock. Poor storage facilities, etc.
All such losses would have to be accounted for in assessing gross takings. The Tribunals have not been consistent in what they will allow under this heading. It all depends on your individual circumstances and how convincing your case is.

i *Private consumption*
This is liable to VAT at cost price and not at the full retail price. So the element of personal drawings from stock must be allowed for in the assessment.

j *Free drinks to staff, draymen, etc.*
Allowances must be made where free drinks are given as legitimate business outgoings.

Finally do remember that you must be able to support any claim or submissions you make with some evidence. This may include not only detailed calculations but also witnesses and witness statements.

CHAPTER EIGHTEEN

Goodbye to all VAT

Cancelling registration/selling a business
Except in the case of successful limited companies whose business life can be virtually limitless, many firms, most partnerships and all sole proprietors will one day be faced with the task of cancelling VAT registration. The circumstances in which registration must be cancelled and those in which cancellation is optional are listed below.

Circumstances in which VAT registration must be cancelled
a Selling all your business to someone else as a going concern.
b Going out of business completely.
c Changing the legal status of the business.
d Ceasing to make taxable supplies (standard and zero rated).
e For intending traders registered before taxable supplies are made—when the intention to make taxable supplies no longer exists.

Circumstances in which VAT registration may be cancelled
When business turnover falls below mandatory registration limits.

Mandatory deregistration

Selling all your business as a going concern to someone else
If you are selling off all your business, you will have to notify your local VAT office who will take steps to cancel your registration. If you are only selling part of your business you will still need to be registered for VAT, if your remaining turnover will exceed £23,600 per annum. Otherwise you may apply for voluntary deregistration (see below).

If you are starting another business immediately, or very shortly after selling your present one, Customs and Excise may allow your existing VAT registration to continue.

When selling off all your business your registration will be officially cancelled, although you may, with the new owner's agreement, transfer your VAT registration number to him, providing he is not already registered. However, in doing so Customs and Excise will insist that all rights and liabilities with regard to VAT amounts outstanding are transferred to the new owner. If you are buying an existing business you should request a new VAT number rather than agree to this procedure. Otherwise you could be buying yourself into a lot of trouble, since no one can guarantee that the previous owner has been truthful in recording his tax liabilities. Even if he may have made genuine innocent errors in the past, you could end up being penalised for them. The dangers involved here far outweigh any administrative conveniences.

Going out of business completely and ceasing to make taxable supplies

If you are going out of business completely, eg because of ill-health, retirement or because business is unprofitable, notify your local VAT office before your last day of trading. They will take steps to cancel your registration.

If you are ceasing to make taxable supplies altogether, eg you may be changing the nature of your business from taxable to exempt by becoming an undertaker, notify Customs and Excise as soon as possible. Your registration must be cancelled.

Changing the legal status of your business

You must notify your local VAT office if the legal status of your business is about to change.

This can happen when:

a   A sole proprietor takes on a partner.
b   A partnership is about to dissolve.
c   A limited company is about to be formed to take over an existing business.
d   A limited company is being wound up.

In each circumstance VAT registration for the old entity will be cancelled and the new entity must register afresh. It is possible to have the old entity's VAT registration number transferred to the new entity if this is desired. Again Customs and Excise insist that the new registration takes on responsibility for the debts of the old. But in circumstances where, say, partners become shareholders in a company which takes over their business, this should present no major problems.

However, where say a company is being wound up owing money to Customs and Excise, it may be advisable to register the new entity taking on the business separately for VAT purposes. This will avoid the transfer of responsibility for the debt to the new entity.

General note

In all circumstances, having once notified your local VAT office of your intentions, they will agree with you a date from which your registration will be cancelled.

From that date you cannot issue tax invoices, so you must ensure that all goods and services sold to customers before the date of deregistration are invoiced on or before the last day of your VAT registration. You cannot claim VAT on goods and services bought after the date of deregistration. If however, you are waiting for tax invoices for services which were engaged before your registration was cancelled, eg solicitor's fees or accountant's fees, you may apply to Customs and Excise to make a special claim.

Stocks and assets

Selling or transferring all or part of your business

If you are selling your business as a going concern, or there is a change of legal entity, you will not be required to account for output tax on any stocks and assets sold or transferred to the new owner. The following conditions must be met for the transfer to be free of VAT.

a   You must be selling all your business, or a part of it that is capable of being run as a separate business.
b   You must complete a record showing the type and value of stocks and assets transferred.

c The stocks and assets you are selling must be relevant to the kind of business you are disposing of.
d The person taking over the business must be registered from or before the date of the takeover of the business.

Be wary if the turnover of your business is close to the VAT registration limits. If the buyer of the business is not already registered he will not be legally obliged to register. If he does not register Customs and Excise will demand from you the VAT on the cash value of your stocks and assets transferred (if the VAT exceeds £250). You must therefore ensure that provision for such an event is written into any contract of sale.

Registration is cancelled but the business is not being transferred

You must make a valuation of any business stocks and assets on hand at the time of deregistration. You can value your stocks at
a Cost excluding VAT;
b Cost of manufacture (for manufacturers only) excluding VAT, and any used assets can be valued at the price you would expect to pay for them (excluding VAT) in their used condition.

Exclude from your valuation:
a Zero rated goods.
b Goods bought from a person who was not registered for VAT.
c Goods on which input tax cannot be reclaimed by law (eg motor cars).
d Goods which you bought before 1 April 1973 on which no rebate of purchase tax or revenue duty has been received.
e Goods directly attributable to exempt outputs.

The value obtained will be the assessable value of standard rated stocks and assets. Calculate 15% of the assessable value. This represents the VAT on stocks and assets on hand at deregistration.

If the VAT amount exceeds £250 you will have to declare the full amount to Customs and Excise on your last VAT return.

The reasoning behind this is that you will have already claimed VAT on your stocks and assets as input tax in past periods. Thus Customs and Excise are recouping VAT that has not moved out of your business.

However, if the VAT on unsold stocks and assets is £250 or less you do not have to declare this as VAT due.

Special note for retailers using scheme E

If you are using retailers' scheme E you will have accounted for output tax on the value of your stocks of goods for resale through the normal operation of the scheme. Do not therefore include the value of those stocks in the above calculation.

Records and accounts

You must keep your records and VAT accounts in the normal manner up to the date of deregistration. Calculate your output tax and input tax up to the final day as you would have done from the date of your last VAT return. Add on to your output tax figure the VAT (if over £250) calculated on the value of your business stocks and assets remaining on hand at the time of deregistration. The VAT office will send you a formal notice of deregistration from VAT and also a final VAT return for the tax period from your last ordinary tax period up to the date of deregistration. Include in this any output tax as calculated above, and the input tax on which you are entitled to relief, and send the return, with the balance due, to Customs and Excise.

Voluntary deregistration

Deregistration limit from 1 June 1989

From 1 June 1989 you are able to apply to be deregistered from VAT if you can satisfy Customs and Excise that your taxable supplies will not be more than £22,600 in the next twelve months.

In working out whether you will exceed this limit or not you should exclude the value of any capital assets which you are going to sell during the period. You should also exclude the amount of VAT itself when counting the value of supplies for deregistration purposes.

Customs and Excise can now limit the extent to which turnover can be manipulated to avoid VAT registration at the margins. They will not cancel a VAT registration if they are satisfied that the reason why turnover will not exceed the deregistration limit in the next twelve months is that either:

a You are going to cease trading (ie making taxable supplies) in that time; or

b You are going to stop making taxable supplies for a period of thirty days or more.

The restriction at **a** prevents a premature cancellation of VAT registration. Otherwise a person carrying on in business and about to cease or transfer his business to someone else could apply to deregister from VAT at a point in time when he realised he only had £22,600 worth of taxable supplies left to make, even if these were all going to me made in the next month or week!

The restriction at **b**, on the other hand, prevents anyone from escaping the VAT net by taking a long holiday of thirty days or more. Some may argue that this takes the anti-avoidance measure too far.

Advantages of voluntary deregistration

The immediate advantage of not being registered for VAT is that you will be saved the time and expense of complying with Customs and Excise requirements, and filling in VAT returns.

You will not be able to charge VAT to customers. Neither will you be able to reclaim it. This could be to your benefit if your customers are members of the public who are not able to claim back VAT.

You will be able to maintain selling prices at the level they were when you were registered which will more than compensate, particularly if your inputs are low in relation to your total outputs.

For example:

	Registered Business		Unregistered Business
	Value	*VAT*	*Value*
Sales (outputs)	10,000	1,500	11,500
Inputs	5,000	750	5,750
Profit to business	5,000	–	5,750

Alternatively you could perhaps afford to let your prices fall somewhat in order to attract further custom.

Disadvantages
If your sales are all, or mainly, of zero rated goods or services you will be at a disadvantage if not registered for VAT. You will not be able to increase the prices of your goods and service and remain competitive with your VAT registered rivals. You will have to bear the VAT on all your purchases of goods and services as a cost to your business.

You will also be at a disadvantage from being unregistered if your customers are all, or mainly, VAT registered. You will not be able to reclaim VAT on the goods and services you buy. If you pass this on as a price increase to a VAT registered customer, he will not be able to reclaim this 'hidden tax' from Customs and Excise. He will prefer to deal with VAT registered suppliers who pass on 'visible' VAT which he can reclaim. You could end up bearing the VAT you pay to your suppliers as a cost in order to remain in business.

Thirdly and finally any stock and business assets that remain unsold by the date of deregistration must be valued as explained earlier in this chapter. VAT must be calculated on your stocks and assets, and, if it exceeds £250, must be paid to Customs and Excise. Thus if you carry valuable stocks or equipment it may be costly to deregister.

Transfer of a business as a going concern

The transfer of business as a going concern between one taxable person and another is not a supply for VAT purposes (remember a taxable person is one who is or should be registered for VAT). Neither is the transfer of a business from a non-taxable person, ie a person not, and not liable to be, registered for VAT, to someone else.

In such circumstances, therefore, the seller should not charge VAT on any stocks and assets or goodwill sold to the buyer as part of the transfer. The seller does not have to transfer all his business to create a VAT free sale, as long as he transfers part of it which is capable of separate operation.

It is a common mistake for the seller of a business in these circumstances to charge the buyer VAT on the valuation of the stock-in-trade. If the buyer is provided with a VAT invoice and claims back the VAT on his next VAT return, Customs and Excise could, on a subsequent control visit, issue an assessment to deny the buyer's claim to input tax. They may quite rightly do so as the VAT was invalidly charged in the first place. They will almost certainly do so if the seller had deregistered from VAT and not accounted for the VAT on his last VAT return. In such circumstances the buyer's only recourse may be to seek recompense from the seller. On buying a business therefore you should ensure that the correct VAT treatment is being applied. Unfortunately, this is not always clear.

Cases have come before the VAT Tribunals in which what was accepted by the seller and buyer as a straightforward sale of assets leased to third parties and not the transfer of a business, was held by the Tribunal panel to amount to the transfer of a business. The VAT guiltlessly charged by the seller to the buyer was denied as a claim to input tax by the latter. If you are in any doubt about the status of a business acquisition you intend to make, seek expert advice and settle the VAT position before you sign on the dotted line. Obtain the views of your VAT office, preferably in writing if there is time.

If you are registered for VAT and you sell your business or part of it you must ensure that certain conditions are fulfilled in order for the transfer to be VAT free:

1. The business must be the whole of your business or a part of it capable of being run as a business on its own.
2. The buyer must be registered for VAT already or he must register for VAT with immediate effect from when the transfer takes place.
3. The assets must be used by the transferee in the same kind of business as carried on by the transferor.

If only one of these conditions fails to be met, the sale of your business amounts to a taxable supply and you will be responsible for accounting for VAT on any standard rated assets, stocks and goodwill sold with the business.

It is a mistake not to charge VAT if the transfer amounts to anything less than the transfer of something which is capable of being run as a business, or if there is no intention on the part of the purchaser to carry on the business as a going concern. If you are in any doubt about either of these facts seek expert advice. If you are in any doubt about your purchaser's intentions obtain a written declaration of intent from him if possible.

If the business you are transferring has a turnover near or below the VAT registration limits check that your purchaser is already registered for VAT before completing the transfer details. If he is not registered find out what his intentions are. You should ensure that your contract of sale includes a provision which allows you to charge VAT to your purchaser if he does not register for VAT, otherwise you may end up paying Customs and Excise VAT out of your sale proceeds.

Transfers of business assets into VAT group registration

From 1 April 1987, when all the conditions governing a VAT-free transfer of business are met, but the assets are acquired by a company which is a member of a VAT group which make exempt supplies (or has exempt input tax in the VAT year) then the VAT group must account for VAT on the taxable assets acquired. It is the representative member's responsibility to account for the VAT to Customs and Excise. In effect it charges itself with VAT. Although the amount of VAT is treated both as output tax and input tax, a partly exempt VAT group may not be able to deduct all the input tax charged to itself under this provision, depending on whether the assets are acquired for making taxable or exempt supplies (for a definition of VAT year and an explanation of Partial Exemption see Chapter 13).

Customs and Excise maintain that the provision is not intended to catch items such as goodwill. It does not apply to items which are not ordinarily chargeable with VAT such as land and buildings, nor does it apply to assets which were acquired by the person transferring the business more than three years before the date of transfer.

The amount of VAT charged in this way is calculated on the open market value of the assets transferred.

Table A

VAT REGISTRATION LIMITS	Annual	[Quarterly]
	[£]	[£]
from 15 March 1989	23,600	8,000
16 March 1988 – 14 March 1989	22,100	7,500
18 March 1987 – 15 March 1988	21,300	7,250

Table B

VAT DEREGISTRATION LIMITS	
Value of taxable supplies in the next twelve months	
	[£]
from 1 June 1989	22,600
from 1 June 1988	21,100
from 1 June 1987	20,300

Index

Abuse of legal powers, 106
Accounts, see Records
Administration, 2–4
Aircraft, 23
Annual accounting, 91–92
Annual VAT return, 90, 93, 94
Appeals, 109
   procedure, 110–115

Bad debts, recovery, 39
Bank statements, 116
Barter-type deals, 30
Betting and gaming, 27
Boats, 23–24
Books, printed matter, 20
Building, construction, 15–16, 21–22
   input tax, 72
   own construction, 76
Burial and cremation, 28
Business, non-business, 72–72
Business entertaining, 73,
   gifts, 31, 75

Calculation of VAT, 29
Capital goods scheme, 85
Caravans, 24
Cars, 72, 74
Cash accounting, 37, 89
Cash and carry, 34–35
Catering, caterers, 19–20, 63–64
Charities
   exemption, 28
   input tax, 71
   zero rate, 24–25
Civil penalties, see Penalties
Claiming back VAT, 71–77, 90
Clothing, children's clothing, 25
Companies:
   group registration, 14
   pre-incorporation input tax claims, 9
   transfer of business, 123–124
Completing returns, 90–94
Connected persons, 30

Construction industry, 21–22
Credit charges, 27
Credit notes, 36
Customs and Excise, 2–4
   powers, 103–106

Debtors, see Bad debts
Default surcharge, 102–103
Deposits, 29–30, 37–38
Deregistration, 119–125
   input tax claims after, 120
   limits, 124–125
Disbursements, 30
Discounts, 30
Distraint, 105–106
DIY builders, 15–16, 76
Drink, 18–20

Education, 27
Entertainment:
   business, 73
   staff, 75
European Community (EC), 2, 18, 20, 21, 43–44
   refunds of VAT from Europe, 77
Exemptions, 1, 4, 25–28
   betting and gaming, 27
   burial and cremation, 28
   charities, 28
   education, 27
   finance, 27
   health, 27
   insurance, 27
   land, 25
   post office, 27
   sports competition, 28
   trade unions and professional associations, 28
   works of art, 29
   see also Partial exemption
Exports, 41–44
   checklist, 42
   personal, 43

False documents, 97
False statements, 97
Finance, 27
Food, 18–20
Footwear, 25
Fraud, 97
Fuel and power, *see* Motoring expenses, Zero rate

Gifts, *see* Business entertaining, Samples
Gross takings, 45–46
Group registration, 14, 124
Guest houses, *see* Hotels

Health services, 27–28
Hotels, 32–33
Houseboats, 24

Imports, 78–81
Inns, *see* Hotels
Input tax
   domestic accommodation, 75
   and exempt supplies, 82–85
Inputs, 4, 71–77, 82–85
Insurance, 27
International services, 22–23
Invoices, 34–36, 72

Journals, *see* Books

Land, 25–26
Liability to VAT, 1, 5, 17–28

Medical aids, 24
Medicines, 24
Mixed supplies, 31–32
Mobile homes, 24
Monitoring turnover, 12–13
Motoring expenses, 73

Newspapers, 20

Offences, 95–97
Ombudsman (Parliamentary Commissioner for Administration), 108
Option to tax (election to waive exemption), 26
Output tax, 5, 93–94
Outputs, 5

Outside the scope, 5
Overseas visitors, 43–44

Pamphlets, *see* Books
Parliamentary Commissioner for Administration (Ombudsman), 108
Partial exemption, 82–85
Payments of VAT, 91
Penalties, 8, 91–92, 95–103
Personal use of business goods, 30
Petrol and derv, *see* Road fuel, Motoring expenses
Pharmacists, 64
Post Office services, 27
Postage and packing, 31
Powers of Customs and Excise, 103–106
Pre-registration purchases, input tax claims, 9
Production of records, *see* Records
Professional bodies, 28
Prosecutions, 95–97

Rates of VAT, 1, 17
Records of accounts, 86–89
Refunds of overseas VAT, 77, 80
Registration,
   before trading, 9
   cancelling, 119–125
   compulsory, 7–8
   divisional, 15
   exemption from, 9, 14
   forms, 8, 10–11
   group, 14–15, 124
   limits, 7–8, 12–13
   overseas persons and residence, 14
   persons not making supplies, 15
   self-help groups, 16
   supplies not liable to VAT, 15
   turnover (taxable supplies), 7–8, 12–13
   voluntary, 9
Repayments, 91
   repayment supplement, 91
Residence, 14
Retail schemes, 5, 45–64
   scheme A, 47–48
   scheme B, 54–56
   scheme B1, 55
   scheme B2, 55–56
   scheme C, 51–54
   scheme D, 49–51

scheme E, 56–58
scheme E1, 58
scheme F, 48–49
scheme G, 58–60
scheme H, 60–61
scheme J, 61–63
  checklist, 47
  retrospective scheme changes, 63
Returns, 90–94
Reverse charge, 5, 80–81
Road fuel,
  invoices, 34–35
  scale charge, 73–74

Samples, 31
Scale charge, *see* Road fuel
Second-hand goods, 29, 65–70
Self billing, 34–35
Self supply, 5, 26–27, 85
Sewerage services, 20
Staff entertainment, 75
Standard rate, 5
Stocks and assets:
  VAT on deregistering, 120–121, 123
Supply, 5

Tax invoices, 34–36
  requirements, 35
  types, 34–35
Tax point, 5, 37–38
Taxable persons, 6

Taxable supply, 6
Trade unions, 28
Transfer of business, 123–124
Transport, 23–24
Tribunals, 109–118
Turnover, 6, 7–8
  monitoring, 12–13

VAT Central Unit (VCU), 2
VAT offices, 2–4
VAT terms, 2–6
VAT returns, 90–94
VAT tribunals, 109–118
VAT visits, 2
Voluntary deregistration, 122–123
Voluntary registration, 9

Water, 20

Zero rate, 1, 6, 18–25
  books, 20
  building, construction, 21–22
  caravans and houseboats, 24
  charities, 24–25
  clothing and footwear, 25
  food and catering, 18–20
  fuel and power, 21
  imports, exports, 24
  international services, 22
  medicines, aids for the handicapped, 24
  transport, 23–24